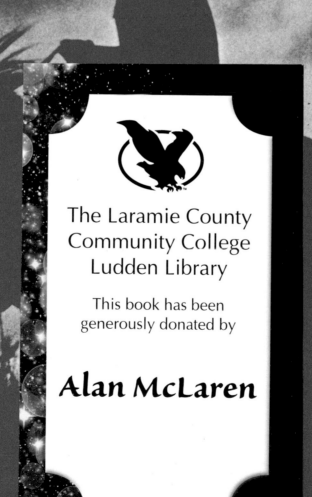

Men of the Saddle

Men of the Saddle

Ted Grant and Andy Russell

*To my man
in the saddle —
I love you —
Martha

Valentine's Day
1979*

VNR Van Nostrand Reinhold Ltd. Toronto
New York, Cincinnati, London, Melbourne

Typesetting by Fleet Typographers Limited
Colour separations by Colourgraph   Reproduction Inc.
Printed by McLaren Morris and Todd Ltd.
Bound by John Deyell Company
Design by Brant Cowie/Artplus Ltd.
All photographs are by Ted Grant
Library of Congress Catalogue Number 77-77629

CANADIAN CATALOGUING IN PUBLICATION DATA

Russell, Andy, 1915–
    Men of the Saddle

ISBN 0-442-29878-1 bd.

1. Cowboys—Alberta.   2. Ranch life—Alberta.
I. Grant, Ted, 1929–   II. Title.

FC3670.C6R88   971.23   C78-001193-7
F1076.R88

---

78 79 80 81 82 83 84 7 6 5 4 3 2 1
Printed and bound in Canada

Published in the United States of America
by Van Nostrand Reinhold Company, New York

For the cowboys we know.

Contents

Author's Foreword

As a boy I grew up in an idyllic setting on a ranch that straddled a place where two valleys come together at the foot of the Rockies in southwest Alberta. It was still frontier country in those days and horses were our only kind of transportation. It seemed as though the smell and the live, warm feel of them was a permanent part of life. I had my first ride on one when I was only a few months over a year old.

I was of the second generation born on the prairies, for my grandfather had come into the country in 1882, when Canada was all wilderness west of eastern Ontario. My father grew up on a ranch cradled in a lovely valley where Pothole Creek joins the St. Mary River a few miles south of where the city of Lethbridge now stands. He rode as a cowboy when there were no fences across the vastness from the Arctic to Texas and beyond. When I was four years old, we moved to the ranch next to the mountains, about sixty miles west as the crow flies. By then most of the country was fenced with barbed wire. The last one was about two miles west of our door. From there you could ride 250 miles before you found another to the west and in a northerly direction there were none.

Around our evening fires I heard stories told by Dad and other riders who had known the country when it was all open range. They were filled with action, adventure and humor, and with a certain flavor of nostalgia. My brother and I helped handle the stock on our ranch, picking up the tricks of riding and roping and learning to handle guns. Ropes, saddles, harness and guns were all tools that were part of our lives and, indeed, our living depended on them. To ride with a frayed cinch was courting disaster or to handle a gun carelessly was to be assured of a blistering reprimand, so we learned to take no chances with things that we used all the time.

Growing up with an interest in the history of the cowboy and the west was more than something merely gathered second hand; it was part of me. Now, when I talk of a bucking horse, it is with easy recall of the storm of pounding saddle leather and powerful muscles when a rider stays on top by confidence and balance. When I speak of picking one's way through a blizzard with the temperature far below zero, it is with the memory of having done so.

To those of us who have been there, smelled the dust under a hot sun and sat a swimming horse in a flooded river, the old paintings of men like Remington and Russell are something more than wonderful art; we relate to them. They are authentic. They froze the action and recorded the most minute details. In a different way, so do Ted Grant's photographs which illustrate this book, only he works in a medium of which Russell and Remington never dreamed. He not only captures the form of tightened muscles, but the texture of skin, the flash of eyes and even the upstanding individual hairs of animals and men. He records the present and at the same instant, the past, for while there have been changes, there are some things that have not changed. Working with high-speed cameras, precision lenses and color film, he is no less an artist, and his pictures are every bit as authentic.

I would like to thank and recognize some very valuable sources from which some fascinating material has been gathered for this book. *Leaves of the Medicine Tree,* written by oldtimers and their descendants from the High River country of Alberta, has been a gold mine of information and material. So has *The Rangemen* by L. V. Kelly, a very rare book of the early history of southern Alberta, long out of print, a copy of which I am lucky enough to own.

We dedicate this book to the oldtimers who pioneered this country, who blazed the trails and gave their lives to build a significant part of Canada and the United States; and to their children and grandchildren who have kept the spirit of freedom and honesty alive in the west.

ANDY RUSSELL

Photographer's Preface

As a boy growing up in the city, cowboys for me were characters in the movies or played out in the back alley with make-believe horses and six-guns. Little did I know that some day I would be riding a horse during a cattle drive, drinking it up and living in a bunkhouse with real cowboys. They do not have six-guns but they do ride tall in the saddle and wear spurs, and like the "good guys" in the movies they all wear light-colored stetsons. To Alec Murdoch, Don Thompson and all those with whom I have had the pleasure to ride, laugh and listen to stories, I offer most sincere thanks for their friendship and the hope that they will enjoy this book as much as I have enjoyed creating it.

There are a few people without whose encouragement the photographs in this book would not exist. To John Ough, former editor of the National Film Board who gave me the first assignment on cowboys, and to Donna and Einar Brasso of Calgary who were the first to sow the seed of the idea for a book, I am especially indebted.

To place the photographs in a framework that would bring them fully to life required a text by an author who knew in the depth of his own soul what it means to be a "real, honest to goodness cowboy." I am fortunate, indeed, to have met just that man in Andy Russell. Amongst his other talents, Andy is one of the great western yarn spinners, and he has written a text that is full of a genuine warmth and authenticity which come from his own experiences as a working cowboy and rancher.

There are many men and boys who dream of being a cowboy and I hope this book will allow them to renew their fantasies, even if only for a few reflective moments.

TED GRANT

Men of the Saddle

Where It All Began

IF YOU RIDE UP ONTO A HIGH HILL a few miles north of Calgary, Alberta, on a clear morning in June, you will be looking at country with sharp contrasts. To the west and southwest, the horizon is sawtoothed with a solid rank of snow-capped peaks, the Rockies—or the Shining Mountains as the oldtime trappers used to call them. Along the front of the mountains is a deep band of foothills with timbered bluffs and grassy slopes. This is cow country, stretching south about 150 miles to the international border; the tenderloin cut of the beef industry of Canada. Too high and rough to be grain country, it is largely grasslands, where men still ride horses in their work and play.

Looking south and east, a vast stretch of spring-green grain fields reaches toward the distant line of the horizon. A hundred years ago, it was the northern edge of a gently rolling ocean of grass broken here and there by ranges of hills. It reached from where you are sitting your horse to the arid cordillera of northern Mexico, and from Lake Winnipeg and the Mississippi River to the Rockies. In those days it was the stamping ground of the buffalo and the first of the oldtime cattlemen and their cowboys: a vast lonely land, hot in summer, cold in winter and infinitely wild.

Here and there in widely scattered places the booming of heavy Sharps rifles marked the end of the immense herds of buffalo that had roamed across the plains for thousands of years before the white men arrived with rifles and wagons on the hunt for new lands and riches. The native Indians watched, angry and baffled at the waste, sometimes taking the war trail in hopeless flashes of rebellion, which were utterly futile in the face of the overpowering numbers of the intruders. It was a time of painful transition that had begun with the early Spanish explorers. It was the sunrise of the relatively short period of time in history, when the cattlemen ruled the range like kings.

It all began back in 1768, when a Spaniard by the name of José de Galvez set out from Mexico with a two-pronged expedition by sea and land for what is now California.

The land expedition was accompanied by mounted soldiers and with them were Mexican peons driving extra horses, pack mules and cattle. Winding slowly across seemingly limitless dry mountains and desert, they pushed their way north and west up around the tip of the Gulf of California, where they forded the wide Colorado River at its mouth. By that time their supplies of food were running low and when they reached their rendezvous with the ships at the coast, their belts were cinched up on lean flanks that seemed to be rubbing on their backbones, their bodies were covered with ugly sores rubbed raw by the chafing of armor, and most of them were suffering from scurvy.

The hunger pangs of the overlanders were eased a bit by food carried on the ships, but they did not rest long before continuing on north. Finally, after more hard going over hundreds of miles of unexplored wild country, they met the boats again at Monterey Bay not far from where San Francisco now stands. There they proceeded to build two missions, San Carlos and San Antonio, in 1771 and 1772.

At first these missions nearly perished, for a drought almost forced the Spaniards to eat their cattle and seed grain. But they managed to hang on by eating jerky made from the meat of the giant California grizzlies, which they killed with either smoothbore flintlock guns or lances. The rains eventually came back turning the country green again, and the wonderfully productive climate joined with the determination of these incredibly tough pioneers to mark the beginning of the golden age of the Californios.

In the green valleys running back from the coast great meadows of lush wild oats waved in the wind and grass lay deep on the slopes under groves of magnificent oak trees. The horses and cattle multiplied, and in 1784 the Governor of Mexico gave the various officers of the military huge land grants on which they set up their own state under the rule of their own Governor. In the meantime they had been joined by their women and built adobe haciendas, rough yet utilitarian headquarters for their huge ranches.

The missions were at the centre of the lives of the Californios. On the mission farms, where fruit, vegetables and grain were cultivated, the hand labor was supplied by numerous Indians who were whipped into submission by the rough hands of soldiers and inducted into the Roman Catholic Church by the priests.

The colony which was thus founded was largely self-sufficient, with its own tanneries, saddle makers and soapworks. Every ranch had its big cast iron soap kettle slung over an open air fireplace. Many of the ranches and missions had their own sawmills run by hand labor with whip saws. Local weavers made blankets and rough cloth from the wool of sheep kept on the missions.

It was the horse that was the key in setting up the Spanish North American empire. The Aztecs had been cowed by these strangers who rode against them on horseback. At first the native Indians too were terrified of the horses, which they called "medicine dogs." But as time went on, the Spanish lost horses, which bred and multiplied in the wild. The Indians soon lost their fear of them and adopted them. By 1750 the plains Indians as far north as Canada were mounted and counted their wealth in horses. In California wild horses increased to such numbers that the Governor passed a decree on several occasions to have thousands of them slaughtered to save the range for cattle.

The Spanish horses of Moorish and Arab blood were the basis of Californio life. Without them this empire of grass and livestock would have been impossible—indeed, the whole history of the conquistadores would have been a blank page. Afoot, the Spaniard was just another man, but on horseback he was something to be reckoned with. In time they passed their skill at horsemanship on to their numerous offspring from Indian women, and these vaqueros became the backbone of the help required on the ranches. The entire life of the Californios was bound up with horses.

The saddles used by the Californios were unique and the first patterns of what we now know as the western type. Sometimes they were richly decorated with hand tooling and silver. Their long, hand-braided reatas made of strips cut from the hides of selected cattle were more than just tools of the range, but weapons that they used sometimes in fights with Indians and often to kill the big grizzlies that roamed everywhere. Their bridles and reins were also plaited from rawhide cut into many strands and worked into intricate designs. Bits and spurs were hand forged from iron and inlaid with silver. The big sombreros that sheltered them from the sun and rain were sometimes made of a kind of wool felt but more often from leather, and these too were sometimes heavily decorated with silver.

When the Californios travelled on business to other ranches or to the missions, each rider had several horses which they drove ahead. When a mount began to tire, a fresh one was roped out of the herd and saddled. Thus it was possible for them to travel great distances in a day. The women rode with the men, for there were no carriages. The only wheeled vehicles they employed were heavy wooden carts drawn by oxen.

Hides and tallow were the major trade items, bartered for such things as iron, silks, spices, weapons and other requirements. The Californios slaughtered their cattle in hundreds at outlying killing grounds called "calaveras"—places of the skulls. They only took the choice cuts of meat, which they dried for their own use, and the hides and tallow. The rest was left for the vultures and the bears.

Grizzlies soon developed a taste for meat and became conditioned to killing cattle. Spanish guns, very crude inaccurate weapons, were inadequate for these mighty adversaries, so whenever possible the Californios caught and killed them with their reatas from horseback. It was a dangerous sport, involving horses and skill, much loved by the Spaniards. They did not, however, come close to wiping out the grizzlies—as a matter of fact, California is the only place in North America where grizzlies increased following the appearance of the white man—but it was exciting and challenging to kill them. Sometimes a horse slipped and fell or a rider got too close to an angry bear and the unfortunate one was badly injured or killed; such tragedies were all part of the game.

These people lived and played on horseback and it was in this way that the rodeo began. To celebrate holidays the Californios would gather, all dressed in their finery, at one of the local ranches. Besides horseracing, there were exhibitions of skill and various games. Stewart Edward White, who was a collector of the history of the Californios, recounts a story of a young caballero intent on making an impression on a beautiful senorita, who was sitting with her family just outside a barrier separating the spectators from the contestants at one of these rodeos. Going to the opposite end of the arena, the young suitor loaded a silver tray with crystal goblets of wine. Mounted on a beautiful horse, with the tray balanced shoulder high on the palm of his right hand, he galloped toward the barrier, jumped the horse over without spilling a drop and proceeded to pass the wine around to the various members of the senorita's family. How many glasses he broke practicing for this trick history does not record.

A popular contest involved taking a rooster and burying it to the neck in the loose sand of the race track. Starting from a mark each contestant rode at a dead run past the rooster and, reaching down from the saddle, attempted to snatch the bird from its hole. It was not easy to do and the rider who managed it was loudly cheered. There were also bull fights and sometimes a fight was staged between a wild bull and a grizzly with money being waged on the outcome. Bets were also placed on battles between fighting cocks.

When the first American free trappers rode into California sometime between 1820 and 1830 from across the mountains to the east, they were not exactly welcomed with open arms by the Californios, but were allowed to winter there. By 1840, when gold was discovered, thousands more poured into the coastal country and Spanish rule came to an end.

Many young Americans found the country to their liking and some settled permanently on ranches. They adopted the comfortable and practical California saddles, learned to use the long rawhide reatas and mimicked some of the dress of the vaqueros. It was here, and in Texas, Arizona and New Mexico, that the early Spanish influence on the equipment and dress of the American cowboy was most evident. Many of the names for various items of equipment illustrate this, for such words as lariat, latigo, rosaderos, chaps and rosettes are of unmistakable Spanish origin. They are still used where cowboys work.

Following the end of the Civil War in the United States, young Texans returned to their frontier home ranges accompanied by other southerners looking for a new start in life. There were thousands of wild cattle roaming in east Texas and all along the Rio Grande River—long-horned and fleet-footed animals that bore little resemblance to the present day beef breeds. Most of them wore no brands and were the property of anyone with the know-how and the nerve to put one on them. It was wild country and a tough place to make a living. Cattle in those days were worth next to nothing—all the cattle in the territory could have been bought after the war for a dollar a head.

But the Union Pacific was pushing a railroad west through Kansas heading toward the Pacific coast. It was about to open a market for beef in the east and enterprising Texans were quick to see the possibilities. There was only the problem of rounding up the cattle and getting them to the end of steel at Abilene.

The Texans built large corrals by burying scrub logs on end in a trench, took a few gentle oxen and prepared for some hard riding. Pursuing and capturing wild longhorns in that broken country covered with scrub oak and other equally ungiving and sometimes thorny growth was no Sunday afternoon picnic. It was hard dangerous work. These cowboys carried short, hard twist, grass ropes, which they tied fast to the pommels of their saddles. Generally they rode in pairs and upon jumping a wild cow or young bull, one rider rode up to it at full gallop and threw a loop over its horns. The other rider would then rope it by the heels and the animal was stretched out between the horses. When it was hogtied, its horns were securely lashed or bolted to one end of a stout beam and the other end was yoked to the neck of a trained ox, which proceeded to head for the corral taking the wild one with it.

Occasionally trap corrals were built around water holes and a number of the wild cattle were captured in that way, but it was never easy. It was a slow hard way to build a herd and more than one man was severely injured or killed in the process. Any old bulls encountered were shot. Every cowboy wore a cap-and-ball six-shooter as insurance in case of a mix-up. The young bulls were castrated and all the cattle were hot-iron branded with the new owner's mark.

Branding was another Spanish contribution to the North American cattle business. But the Spaniards can take no credit for inventing it, as hot-iron branding had been used in Britain at the time of the Roman occupation and the Egyptians had used this method to identify their animals over 4000 years ago, as is recorded on the walls of their tombs.

Catching wild cattle was one thing but keeping them from taking to the brush at the first opportunity was another. Texas cowmen solved this problem by stitching the animals' eyes shut with a needle and thread. Thus blinded temporarily, the cattle could still water and feed sufficiently to stay alive. By the time the stitches had rotted out, they had been slowly moved to strange ground by trailing them behind oxen that wore bells around their necks. In the process the cattle learned to take some comfort in close association with their own kind and had grown to respect and respond to mounted men. And so it was that those first trail herds were lined out towards Abilene in Kansas.

Once trail broken, the herd could be handled with relative ease by the cowboys. But the riders had little chance to relax or to accumulate any fat on their lean hard frames. There were rivers to cross, with quicksand and deep water. Hostile Indians sometimes swooped in close, attempting to stampede the cattle or collect some scalps. Buffalo herds on the move sometimes became mingled with the cattle and scattered them. Prairie fires were a menace to be feared and avoided.

Most of all, perhaps, the cowboys dreaded the possibility that in the dead of night something would frighten the herd off its bedground and into a wild stampede in the dark. There was nothing worse to handle and bring under control than a bunch of cattle stampeding in a wild panic at night. As I once heard an old cowboy say, "The ones in front go like hell, plumb afraid the ones behind are goin' to run over them, and the ones behind run like hell to keep up!" The only way to stop it was by bending the leaders one way or another to turn the herd back into itself in a milling circle. Then, when they had run short of wind, they could be stopped. But at best, it melted the fat off them and the cost was high.

Sometimes the riders shot a few of the leaders to make the rest swing around. They had to ride at top speed and with every jump their horses made their lives were in jeopardy. If a horse tripped and fell, both man and mount were generally trampled into bloody rags by the herd. Many a cowboy was buried on the prairie with very little ceremony except the uncovered heads of the survivors and perhaps a few spoken words remembered from childhood days of Bible learning. Sometimes a wagon tailgate with the luckless one's name carved on it was the only marker. Just as often the grave was left unmarked. It was a sad and sorry event that left many cowboys shaking in their blankets at night as they remembered and wondered how long it would be before their turns came.

There was usually one cowboy to about every 100 head of cattle on a trail drive. So a herd of 1500 head would have had a crew of fifteen to twenty men, a trail boss and a cook, who rode the chuckwagon hitched behind four head of horses or mules. Generally there was an additional rider who served as nighthawk, the horsewrangler whose job it was to keep the extra saddle horses handy for the crew.

In the morning the herd was strung out in a long line off the bedground with a rider on point to pick the way. Behind him other riders rode along the flanks of the herd and two brought up the rear or "drag" as it was called. This was an unenviable position, for it meant pushing the slow cattle and enduring an unending cloud of dust. On dry stretches this dust cloud could be seen for miles. The pace of the cattle was set by a lead steer, usually a big, gentle animal that was a natural leader. They were herded slowly and learned to graze as they went so they would put on weight.

Such a herd was but a speck on the immensity of prairie—a sea of grass deep enough in places to touch the stirrups of the riders—a vast sweep of gold and green reaching to the horizon in every direction. Occasionally there was a break in it, where big cottonwoods grew along the banks of the rivers. Everything that walked, crawled or flew across the prairie was directly or indirectly dependent on the grass, something that has not changed, for if the grasses of the world were wiped out today by some virulent plague, most everything would die out with them.

Small as they were, compared to the scene in which they walked, those first herds going north from Texas were the wedge driven in the door of the old kingdom of nature in North America's plains country. Ranching and farming could not have been established with the herds of buffalo and other game that had lived there for thousands of years in numberless herds. While the protein units per square mile growing on the great plains were likely higher then than they have ever been since, the transition was in the making.

The cowboys that trailed with those herds were opening the next chapter of history following those made by the explorers, the free trappers and the fur trade. Like the trappers, the cowboys were the product of their environment, tough, often ruthless, but sometimes very mild and gentle. They had their own code of life and they worked where the rule was the survival of the fittest. Those who could think for themselves and move skillfully and fast in tight spots were the ones who lived long enough to get old.

They were a potpourri of southern culture. Some were well educated, from aristocratic families who had seen their estates wiped out in the turmoil of the Civil War. Some were farm boys looking for adventure. Others were drifters, illiterate flotsam and jetsam tossed aside by the war. Among them were outlaws seeking far places where they were not known. All were horsemen, centaurs in the saddle where a man afoot would have been nothing in the great sea of grass.

Like all horsemen, they were a proud breed. For the most part they were poor in possessions and rich in experience although young in years. The scale of pay largely followed the price of steers—an average of forty dollars a month, which was what a steer brought at the railhead. Each man owned a saddle, rope, rain slicker and bed made up of blankets rolled in a waterproof canvas tarp. This bed was called a sougan. Extra clothes and a few personal possessions were carried in a sack called a war-bag. Every man carried a six-shooter on a leather cartridge belt slung around his waist. It was often said that in the morning, before eating some breakfast and saddling up for the day's work, the first thing a man put on was his hat and the last, his gun. Most of them carried a rifle in a scabbard slung butt forward under the left stirrup leather out of the way of his rope. In this vast territory there was no law, so firearms were essential equipment. In the event of a dangerous mix-up with an angry cow or an outlaw horse, a six-shooter and knowing how to use it was often the only way to stay alive. Just the same, most cowboys were by no means the weapon-burdened hardcases pictured in popular belief. To be sure there were quarrels that were settled by guns, and there were many incidents in which guns were used in a most irresponsible fashion, but for the most part guns were just another tool used for survival.

The Colt six-shooter has been dramatized by Hollywood to a ridiculous point. Ironically, however, anyone who ever owned one and who had any sense of self-preservation always carried an empty chamber under the hammer making it a five shot gun. If a six-shooter falls out of a holster or is accidentally dropped, it almost invariably turns over and comes down on the hammer, and the weight of it shears off the sear allowing the discharge of the gun if it is fully loaded. More than one man has accidentally shot himself with a loaded six-shooter in this fashion. In one story, a man on the hurricane deck of a bucking horse had his pistol thrown out of the holster, and it went off as it struck the ground. When the dust settled, he retrieved his gun and in due course discovered a .45 calibre hole through the brim of his hat close to his head.

Those first herds that broke trail from Texas to Abilene were just the beginning of a great movement of cattle. Following Abilene, Dodge City became the main terminal. More and more herds came north until sometimes there were several big outfits holding their cattle on the grass as close to the shipping pens as possible, waiting their turn. Southern cattlemen and eastern businessmen saw the opportunities afforded by the vast expanses of grass in Colorado, Wyoming, North and South Dakota and Montana. Big ranching holdings were set up with cattle driven north from Texas as well as east from Oregon and Washington. By the late '70s and early '80s all of the western States and a good part of western Canada was grazing cattle. As yet there were no barbed wire fences.

The Canadian prairies were the last to be settled and the first cattle came north across the boundary from the United States. Naturally, the cowboys came with them, but as the industry expanded, their ranks were swelled by young men from Britain and the eastern provinces of Quebec, Ontario and the Maritimes. Most of these had grown up with horses and it did not take them long to learn the skills and adopt the garb. The famous cowboy artist and writer, Will James, was a French Canadian born in Quebec who took the name of James after he came west.

As mentioned before, cowboy equipment following the influence of the Spanish originated in the United States. Saddles from Texas favored the rimfire, double rig—with two cinches. These saddles had a low horn designed for a tied rope. The riders who used them carried grass ropes thirty to forty-five feet long.

California saddles were higher in the cantle and had a horn designed for dallying. Riders with these saddles carried sixty- to seventy-foot, braided, rawhide ropes that were strong but would not stand a sudden jerk. When one of them swung a big loop to catch a steer, he took wraps on his saddle horn so he could let it give when the animal took up the slack; it was a bit like playing a fish on a line. These saddles were generally full-flower carved and some were decorated with engraved, sterling silver conchas, cantle rims and other trimmings. Some had long, pointed tapaderos hung on the stirrups, and saddle pockets with long covers trimmed with bear or seal fur.

The Texans generally used leather chaps to protect their legs from cactus and brush, while the California cowboys wore chaps made from bear and sealskin. Cowboys east of the mountains adopted angora goat skin for their chaps, which were better for the rain and the cold northern winters.

Almost every big cow outfit had its fashion leader. These nearly all favored the California rigging whether or not they came from that part of the world. It was something to see a long-backed rider sitting a fine big horse in full regalia of this kind. Foremen were inclined to be suspicious of the fancy Dan riders, but some of them were top hands. As one oldtimer put it, "Yuh never can tell how far a frog can jump by just lookin' at him!" Even if these riders were inclined to admire their own shadows as they rode, they certainly added color to their surroundings and you could see the sun reflecting off them for miles.

Cowboys have a weakness for "horse jewelry"—bridle bits and spurs forged in many designs. Some were plain and some beautifully inlaid with silver. Almost universally they wore big, felt hats as protection from the rain and sun. The cowboy hat has become the hallmark of the west and is now worn by many who don't know a cantle from a frying pan and couldn't ride a horse through a gate. The cowboy boot evolved from cavalry boots and in early days had undershot heels sometimes two and a half inches high. The tops were closed and reached to just under the knee, and were often stitched in intricate design and color. This kind of boot was strictly for riding and terrible for walking any distance.

A slicker made from linen or heavy cotton treated with cod liver oil was standard equipment. In nice weather it was carried tied behind the cantle with the skirt hanging on the right side. This garment was cut in such a way that it covered the rider, his saddle and the coiled lariat.

Cowboy clothing was largely utilitarian and often ragged and dirty. Working with cattle and horses is not clean work. The man that would have been horrified to find his horse a host to lice was sometimes lousy himself. Oldtime bunkhouses were considered luxurious if the roof didn't leak; they were usually made of logs chinked with grass and mud—ideal havens for human lice and bedbugs. It was not unusual to see a cowboy pounding the seams of his shirt between two rocks to discourage the livestock hiding there.

The way a man dressed had no bearing on his rank in any cow outfit; he was judged on his skill and ability to get things done. The foreman was at the top of the hierarchy in a working crew. Next to him was the rough rider, or bronc stomper as he was sometimes known, the man who could ride the horses too rank for the average cowboy. He might be ugly as sin, illiterate as a bear and smell like a goat, but if he could hold down his job, he earned ten dollars a month extra. He also got special recognition among his fellows. Such men, if they survived, usually ended up bent and crippled from numerous injuries over the years. Topping off the rough horses was a good way to keep from getting old.

The most important man on any cow outfit was the cook, for the whole operation was enhanced if he was good. He might be the crankiest, most ornery and miserable individual for many miles, but if he turned out light, fluffy biscuits, good stew and other tasty food, the whole crew bragged him up to the sky. An outfit might have a reputation for being mighty tough to work for, but if its cook was good there was no shortage of hands.

Although noted for being crotchety and temperamental, the odd cook had a sense of humor. There is a story about one who was working in a remote line camp one spring. The weather was very wet, every coulee was swimming deep and the rivers were impassable. Supplies were running low and about all he had to feed his crew were beans. A hungry stranger rode in unexpectedly and asked if he could have something to eat. "Sure thing," said the cook. "We got thousands of things to eat—all of 'em beans!" and proceeded to ladle out a plateful from a big kettle simmering on the stove.

The first American cattlemen to reach Canada migrated north into British Columbia from Washington. In 1862, a man by the name of John Park trailed a herd up the Okanagan Valley to the summit leading west through the Kamloops country. Proceeding by way of Williams Lake, he turned north to the Cariboo gold fields, where he sold his beef.

On his way he rode through virgin country where the grass was flank deep to a four-year-old steer. Returning south, he gathered up another herd and returned to set up a ranch on the Bonaparte River valley just a few miles west of Cache Creek in a truly beautiful location—a ranch that is still owned by his grand nephew, Gordon Park. This was the first big ranch set up in the famed Cariboo ranching country of British Columbia.

When the western States were settled, it was largely a lawless land with no real recognition of its status in the country beyond possession. Consequently settlement there was fraught with violence—

Indian wars, range wars and considerable outlaw activity. Men carried the law in a holster slung on a cartridge belt around their hips.

When American cattlemen came north into the Canadian prairie they found a different atmosphere. There the North West Mounted Police (later the Royal Canadian Mounted Police) had come first to establish law and order before the settlers showed up. They were a small but well-trained military group that quickly won the respect of the Indians as well as the white man. They were tall, fearless men who wore distinctive and colorful uniforms. Charlie Russell, the famous cowboy artist, called them the Queen's war hounds. There is a story that one early American settler who trailed a bunch of cattle into the Fort Macleod region left his only spare pair of pants unattended in his wagon. An Indian came along and appropriated the pants, which upset the rightful owner very much. He rode into the Fort and braced Colonel Macleod with a request for permission to shoot any Indians he caught prowling around his outfit. That worthy officer fixed him with cold blue eyes and assured him that anybody who shot an Indian would be arrested, tried and subsequently hanged.

The cowboy who showed up in any settlement in western Canada wearing a gun with the intent of generally hoorawing and terrorizing the public at large was quickly relieved of it and if he ever saw it again it was sheer accident. The Mounted Police were firm, fair and strict. Early ranchers found western Canada a peaceful territory as a result, a place where they could concentrate on business without having to spend time and energy protecting themselves from hostile Indians and roaming outlaws.

Following the disappearance of the buffalo, the cattle business in Canada grew fast but was limited to contracts for beef with Indian agencies and a thin scattering of settlements. One rancher by the name of Shaw made history in 1874, the same year that the Mounted Police arrived, by driving 500 beef cattle east from Tobacco Plains on the Kootenai River in British Columbia. He crossed the Rockies—probably through the Crow's Nest Pass— a distance of over 100 miles through some of the most rugged mountains on the continent and wintered his cattle near Morley before heading north for Edmonton.

In 1884 the Canadian Pacific Railway reached Fort Macleod and this changed the whole horizon of the beef industry. The range was still open with no barbed wire fences from the North Pole to Texas and cattle dotted the plains in the wake of the vanished buffalo.

In Alberta, the ranchers located their headquarters in sheltered places close to wood and water. Line riders were employed at outlying camps to keep the cattle wearing various brands as close to their respective home ranges as possible. But mixing of the herds was inevitable, so each spring a roundup was held under the direction of a captain chosen by the ranchers involved. Each rancher sent representative cowboys and each rider had about ten mounts with him; the number of representative riders depended on the size of the herd involved. Each roundup crew had one or sometimes two or more chuckwagons and cooks. The horse herd or remuda was in the charge of a wrangler.

Every morning at daylight, the night wrangler drove in the remuda, sometimes numbering 200 saddle horses or even more, and they were corralled in a rope corral generally made of just one strand of rawhide strung from stakes about three and a half feet from the ground. These stakes were braced to the outside, the rope held tight by guy lines to shorter ones. A couple of the best ropers of the outfit caught the horses chosen by the riders as their first mounts of the day. These ropers never swung their ropes, but generally lifted them with a sweeping motion from behind. Occasionally, if the horse was heading to the left, the rope was swung once in a back-handed flip, the hoolihan, for the catch. This trick is practiced by very few ropers today. When the horses had been caught and saddled there were generally a few that bucked the kinks out of themselves and their riders, some action usually accompanied by good-natured cheering or raillery, depending on the rider's ability to stay on top.

Then the roundup captain took his crew up on top of the nearest high ground and sent them off in pairs in various directions to comb the country for cattle. Meanwhile, the cook drove his chuckwagon ahead to a designated spot and set up camp. By midafternoon, the cattle began coming in to be held until all the riders arrived and then the branding of calves got under way. The top ropers were picked to heel the calves. The large part of the crew was divided into pairs to throw them and hold them down, while they were branded, castrated and earmarked. As the ropers dragged the calves to the branding fire where the irons were kept hot, they called the brand of the cow it was following and thus each ranch was able to mark their cattle. In cases of disputed ownership, the roundup captain was called to settle the matter. It was up to the riders to see that their home ranches got fair treatment. The work went swiftly and often 200 to 300 calves were branded in a matter of two or three hours. The hours were long and it was hot, hard work well laced with sweat, the smell of burning hair, dust and action.

Sometimes the cowboys were young. My father rode "rep" for his father's brand when he was only sixteen. He got no favors for his youth and expected none. He told of one youngster by the name of Elderidge who was only fourteen, a tough, hard-riding, cheeky kid, who could ride and rope as well as the average hand. There was nothing retiring about him and one day the foreman and one of the riders bent him over the wagon tongue to give him a sound spanking with a pair of chaps and teach him some manners. The licking did nothing but make him smoulder. That night he was night herding close to camp and crept in to slip the loop of his rope around the foreman's feet as he lay asleep. Before that worthy gentleman knew what was up, he found himself bouncing out across the prairie behind a running horse. The kid refused to turn him loose until he had apologized and promised no retribution. Then, under a high moon, the foreman walked back to camp, barefoot, gathering up various belongings on the way.

Roundup crews could handle a great many cattle in a month and by the end of the spring drive very few calves were left that did not wear a brand. The ones that were missed were called mavericks and more than one rancher got his start by putting his brand on such cattle. However, it was a practice that was frowned upon and viewed with suspicion.

In the fall a similar roundup was staged to gather the beef—the annual cut of prime, grass fat, four-year-old steers. These were slowly trailed to the nearest railway shipping point and sold for market use. These animals were handled very carefully so there would be a minimum loss of fat, or "shrink" as it is still called. Any herder that was careless enough to strike a match to light a smoke at night and let the foreman see him was almost sure to be fired on the spot. The sudden flutter and flare of an old-fashioned sulpher match on the edge of a bedground at night was enough to trigger the cattle into an instant run.

The night watches were divided into three-hour stints and usually entailed two or three riders, who rode slowly around the bedded cattle singing as they went. Whether or not a cowboy had a good voice didn't seem to matter; it kept the cattle quiet nonetheless. The songs they sang had come up the trail from Texas, sometimes mighty sad and doleful ballads of unrequited love and death on the prairie. It was not a bad job in good weather but no fun in a storm. Then the night guard was often doubled and occasionally, if the cattle started to drift, the whole crew would be riding.

As always, the cowboys lived in dread of a stampede. My father told of one when 400 big, fat steers blew up in a thunderstorm and lit out for the horizon. The cowboys got them turned about five miles from camp and at daylight the herd was milling around the top of a low butte bawling dismally with the steam towering over their backs. The foreman sat his horse rolling a smoke and softly remarked, "By God! I'd like to have all the money that's gone up in that steam!"

It was in bad winter storms that cattle sometimes drifted clear out of the country. In the hard winter of 1906 and '07, when blizzards howled almost continuously and the temperatures dropped to forty below zero, thousands of cattle died. Some of those that survived from around the Lethbridge country drifted away down into Montana—some so far east along the banks of the Missouri River that the owners just sold them where they were, when they found them in the spring.

There might be romance attached to being a cowboy, especially the Hollywood version, which has been responsible for a lot of distorted ideas expounded by people who don't know, but it was truly a very tough life. Some writers today class them as being underpaid, ignorant and violent men, "who fried their brains under the sun" and had little more intelligence than their cattle. Those writers simply don't know the breed. Arrogant they were, and somewhat arrogant they still are, but for the most part they were real men, loyal almost to a fault, ready for anything anytime and basically honest—no man ever had better friends. In truth, no man ever had better neighbors on this earth. When the chips were down, you could count on them. What more can anyone say for any man?

It is easy to understand why the cowboy was an important part of the beef industry in those early days on the prairie. Without these hard-riding, skillful men, who took such pride in being what they were, this frontier era of the business would not have been possible. They cut out for themselves a most unforgettable part of our history.

Some Hazards of the Game

IN THE EARLY DAYS OF RANCHING on the open range, where thousands of cattle ran free, there was no way for a foreman and his crew of cowboys to keep constant contact with the stock wearing their ranch's brand. But they kept their cattle on their chosen range as much as possible, at the same time watching for rustlers and four legged predators, as well as keeping an eye on any bogs dangerous to cows. These were problems common to all and there was cooperation practiced in controlling them, just as there is today.

From the earliest days rustling was always of concern to the ranchers. The native Indians had seen the buffalo herds wiped out in ten years—herds that had provided them with a bounteous living for thousands of years—and the transition of being confined to reservations following the signing of the 7th Treaty in 1877 was traumatic. They were hunters cut off from their old, free-wandering ways, suddenly dependent on handouts from the white man. Being proud and independent people, they not only felt the loss keenly but understandably resented it. Small wonder that they occasionally killed a fat heifer or steer for meat, for that was the way they had lived for countless generations. Some ranchers hated them for their depredations; others accepted the losses as part of living in the country. The Mounted Police did a salutary job of keeping the peace.

The cowboys riding the prairies in the employ of the ranchers had some sympathy for the Indians, for they were half-wild, free-roaming men themselves with a certain understanding of their native brothers. To be sure, many cowboys looked down on the Indians, but when they found evidence of a cow being killed they sometimes looked the other way. In a land where white women were scarce, for some men there was welcome in the teepees and the affection of a girl with long, braided black hair and sparkling eyes. While there was a measure of joy in such romances, there was also sadness, for the girls were vulnerable to the blandishments of these dashing, handsome young men. Except on rare occasions, there was no future for the girl involved except the possibility of a papoose with blue eyes.

Occasionally a homesteader too, with a sod shanty full of hungry children, killed a beef cow, but it was organized rustling that really hurt the ranchers and posed a real problem for the Mounted Police. While their horseback patrols covered an enormous amount of country, they were few in number and the backgrounds of most of the men in the force did not give them the kind of experience needed in dealing with these thieves. But in spite of their many other duties, they tried hard to cope with rustling rings. Special stock detectives were sometimes employed, men with backgrounds in the cattle business who worked in plain clothes. However, there were few of them and quite often they were far away when needed.

A member of the Mounted Police told me a story of the dilemma faced by a rookie who had been assigned to an area where rustling was something to be dealt with. For reasons that will become obvious I cannot give his real name, so we will call him Jim. In the early 1930s Jim was assigned to a large district in southeastern Alberta, a vast, semi-arid country where the rustling of cattle and horses back and forth across the international border was extremely common. His experience as a police officer was short, but he was longer on knowing something about livestock, being ranch raised.

In between routine duties, Jim rode far and wide across the prairie and through the hills trying to gather concrete evidence of the rustling. He was sure that it was being practiced by several ranchers working in an organized group. Outwardly they appeared to be leading exemplary lives, but from bits and scraps of information, Jim was convinced of some mighty "fishy" activity, although he had nothing solid to pin on them. Reports of missing livestock continued to come in from various sources and his superior officer was getting more and more restive.

One day as he was riding past a set of corrals at a little prairie loading station along the railroad he noticed something. The corrals were being used as a sort of community branding facility and the brands of most of the ranchers in the district were neatly hung on nails along the inside of the top rail of the main pen near the gate. The sight of the irons gave him an idea. It was a highly unethical—even illegal—idea but Jim had a wild hair or two of his own, and the humor of it appealed to him. He knew that if he were ever found out, he would be in big trouble. He would need some luck.

A rodeo was due to be held in a few days, so he waited until almost everybody was away enjoying the celebration at Medicine Hat. At dawn that morning, he was out on his best horse scouting the country around the pens before beginning to round up all the loose horses he could find in the vicinity. By midmorning he had quite a bunch in the corrals and was pleased to note that the spring colts were as yet unbranded.

He built a fire out of scrap wood lying around the corrals, heated the irons required and went to work. He used up most of the rest of the day roping colts, throwing them and tying them down and branding them. He used one suspect's brand on horses belonging to another. With some considerable art, he even altered some of the brands on the colts' mothers. In short, he raised some particular kind of hell, all the while keeping a wary eye out for any approaching riders. Had he not been a strong man and an excellent roper, the job would have been impossible. When he had finished to his satisfaction, he hung up the irons and tidied up a bit before turning the horses loose. Then he rode for home.

When the ranchers discovered the switched and altered brands there was a terrific uproar. Somebody had been playing mighty bold with their horses. But who? Nobody suspected that a Mounted Police officer would ever do such a thing. There was a lot of narrow-eyed, suspicious talk as Jim went around doing his duty trying to track down the careless customer who had wielded the irons. Needless to say, it remained one of the unsolved cases on police files. None of the suspects ever quite trusted the others again and the rustling stopped. They knew that somebody was aware of what had been going on and with the finger of suspicion pointing in all directions, it was a wise conclusion.

This was a fine example of fighting fire with fire. It saved the taxpayers a lot of money and was effective. Twenty years later Jim was still laughing about it. "For a bunch so damn fast and loose about what they did with other people's stock, they were sure some fussy!" Jim opined as he wound up his story.

One of the first stock detectives hired by the Mounted Police was Jack Reid, a product of the frontier and son of Bill Reid, who was wagon master at the famous Wagon Box fight near Fort Phil Kearney in Wyoming, when a large band of Sioux warriors under Red Cloud made the mistake of jumping a small contingent of cavalry and wagon drivers hauling wood to the fort. Although history is hazy about who was responsible for that victory, it was Bill Reid's drivers armed with the new repeating Henry .44 rifles and two Colt revolvers apiece using the same ammunition that were the strength. Sheltered by their wagons loaded with logs and upset in a circle, they poured a withering fire into the attacking Indians. The cavalrymen were still armed with .45-70 single shot Springfields that had the nasty habit of jamming when fired fast. Bill Reid was also scout for the 7th Cavalry when they took a beating at the Battle of the Rosebud, and one of the first on the scene after the massacre of Custer's force on the Little Bighorn.

Jack Reid was raised on the family ranch on the Little Missouri not far from Teddy Roosevelt's holding near Medora, North Dakota. He came to Alberta near the beginning of World War I and found employment as foreman wintering a bunch of beef steers on the Bow River for Pat Burns. Rustlers were operating in the area and in due course they chose to kill three steers in Jack's care. He did some riding and looking, which led him to suspect two brothers living on a small ranch nearby. Not far from their place he found the hides of the butchered steers, with the brands cut out, hidden in a draw. A short distance away, the severed heads were located in a deep washout.

One of the steers was a "marker," a brindle with some white spots. Its hide could be admissible evidence on the testimony of several men who knew it, but such evidence was shaky without the brands. So Jack proceeded to watch until one day the bachelor brothers left home and headed for Calgary.

Accompanied by one of his cowboys, he rode to their buildings to have a look around. Without a police officer and a search warrant such a maneuver had its definite limitations, and as he sat his horse in the middle of the yard, asking himself where the suspects would likely conceal three pieces of hide with the damning brands, his eyes came to fall upon the outhouse. Dismounting, he walked over and entered it and a minute later he called his rider.

When the cowboy came to the door of the "john", there was Jack with a lighted match in his hand peering down the hole in the seat, and he called attention to the fact that the waste below looked as if it had been recently disturbed. It didn't take long for them to find a shovel, upset the outhouse and begin digging. Sure enough, this brought the three patches of hide to light and some application of water revealed the brands.

Charges were laid and in due course the case came to court. Jack presented his evidence by fitting the pieces of hide and heads together like a jigsaw puzzle right there on the floor of the courtroom in front of the judge—a somewhat odious business in the heated room full of people. Everyone, including the thieves, was likely glad when it was over. The rustlers confessed and were given a stiff sentence. The Mounted Police were so impressed that they offered Jack a job as stock detective, which he accepted, and he was instrumental in breaking up several rustling rings.

Ranchers of the Maple Creek region of Saskatchewan were suffering mysterious losses of cattle and every effort to find the thieves had been fruitless, so Jack was sent to work on it. He was supplied with money to lease a small ranch and stock it with cattle. As usual, he wore no uniform and posed realistically as a cowman starting up his own operation. He worked hard, got acquainted with his neighbors, listened to talk and watched. Months went by and in due course the finger of suspicion pointed toward a rancher named Schultz, who not only owned some land and cattle but also a butcher shop in town.

Jack made his acquaintance and found him a dour, taciturn man not given to being very friendly with anyone. But they had one thing in common, a love of guns, and this opened a road to better relations. Jack found that Shultz regularly carried a fine, German Luger, semi-automatic pistol in a shoulder holster. He also learned that Shultz had formerly ranched near Shelby, Montana.

On the pretext of buying some more cattle, Jack went to Montana to do some backtrailing. Inquiry uncovered the interesting information that Shultz's reputation there also pointed to suspected rustling, although nobody had ever pinned it on him. It also revealed that he had hired a young cowboy, who was very well liked, and who subsequently had been dragged to death at the end of his own rope which had been tied solid to his saddle horn. What aroused suspicion about this supposedly accidental death was the fact that the victim had been known to be a fine roper who never tied his rope. Murder was suspected. Perhaps the cowboy had discovered something and quarreled with his boss. Anyway, feelings had run high, and Shultz had disappeared. Jack did some more careful searching and located some of the cowboy's relatives, who were able to supply a small photo of the young man, and there his search ended.

Returning to Saskatchewan, Jack bided his time for several months watching his cattle, mostly at night. One night under a full moon two riders showed up and cut out several big steers, which they drove away. Keeping out of sight, Jack trailed them for several hours and they eventually led him to a pen back of Schultz's butcher shop. There he arrested the butcher and the two cowboys in the act of butchering one of the steers. They were a tough, close-mouthed trio and refused to answer any questions, so Jack left them in custody of the Mounted Police and headed for Schultz's ranch, arriving there about breakfast time.

When Schultz came out of his cabin to greet him, the slight bulge of the shoulder holster under his jacket was evident. Jack was also wearing his .44-40 Colt six-shooter in a shoulder holster. He was alert and wary as he carefully reached into his shirt pocket, and without saying a word he handed Schultz the photograph of the cowboy he had probably killed.

Schultz took one look at it, turned pale and stiffened as though about to reach for his gun. Jack had him pinned with the coldest grey eyes imaginable, and his hand was poised within inches of his gun as he said, "You are under arrest for stealing cattle." Schultz remained frozen for a moment longer, then wilted and Jack took him into town to join his crew.

The rustlers were all sentenced to two years in penitentiary. When Schultz was finally released, he was only a shell of his former self. He holed up in an old, abandoned cabin in the Cypress Hills and died there a few months after.

When Jack told me this story years later, he remarked that Schultz had undoubtedly lived in constant fear of arrest for murder and the worry had killed him. It was a kind of indirect justice for a killing that he had committed.

Though he was many years my senior, Jack Reid and I were great friends and he eventually gave me the Colt revolver that he had carried for so many years as a cowboy and stock detective. I still have it—a reminder of a real frontiersman gone now over the great divide.

When the buffalo were wiped out, the prairie lobo wolves turned to beef and their depredations were something to keep a rancher awake at night. The cattlemen hired wolfers, many of them men who had hunted down the buffalo, and paid bounty on the wolf scalps taken by them. Thousands of wolves were poisoned with strychnine planted in the carcasses of cattle and many were trapped or shot. Some ranchers kept packs of big, specially bred and trained hounds to run them down. Teddy Roosevelt told of such hunts in which he took part in North Dakota, when he was a young man.

At times the cowboys pursued the wolves on horseback and roped them. My father told me of such an incident, when he and another cowboy jumped two big wolves off a cow they had just killed near the

Little Bow River. Both wolves were stuffed with meat and slow, so they had no trouble roping one, which they killed. Meanwhile, the other wolf had time to regurgitate its belly full of beef, and when they rode in pursuit of it they were left far behind in the rough country alongside the valley.

Anytime the cowboys found a wolf den with pups in it, they shovelled them out and destroyed them. George Lane of the Bar U Ranch and some of his crew jumped a family of wolves close to their den one day near High River. The parents fled but the halfgrown pups dove into the den. The cowboys were in something of a dilemma, for they had no shovel, and knew that if they left the den the parents would come back and move the pups. But then they spotted a freight train coming along the track half a mile away. George rode out and flagged it down, borrowed a shovel from the fireman, and they proceeded to dig out the den while the train waited. Freight trains were obviously not in much of a hurry in those days.

Thus the wolves were wiped out, but some of them survived in the foothills and mountains. Even today, a pack occasionally shows up in ranching country and losses have been reported in the Porcupine Hills of southwest Alberta as recently as the winter of 1976-77.

Grizzlies once roamed the prairies as far east as Lake Winnipeg and the Mississippi River. They were, as today, largely vegetarian, but also preyed on the buffalo—to a large extent crippled ones and those killed by wolves. When the buffalo disappeared, the hide hunters turned to hunting the big bears for their skins. There is a record of 1500 grizzly pelts being taken in trade in 1874 by one trader just east of the Cypress Hills. Thus harried, a few surviving prairie grizzlies holed up in the foothills and mountains of southwest Alberta and there are still some cattle killed by them. A full account of the depredations of grizzlies in Alberta ranching country and the adventures of ranchers who hunted and trapped them would fill a large book.

The grizzly's love of carrion moved them to clean up carcasses dead from accident or disease and caused them to be blamed for many dead animals they had not killed. Many ranchers developed a kind of paranoia about bears in general and as a result killed them at every opportunity. But the fact remains, very few grizzlies ever learn to kill cattle.

One job the oldtime cowboy did not enjoy was riding the bogs in spring. In many parts of the country there were numerous sinkholes, bottomless bogs of slippery, slimy muck, where the grass became green earlier than elsewhere. Cattle were sometimes trapped in these bogs and it was necessary for patrolling riders to pull them out. The easiest way to do it was to ride up within throwing distance and drop a loop over the trapped animal's horns and drag it out. This unceremonious treatment often made a cow very angry and the cowboy found the hardest part of the job was turning it loose.

One spring when I was about twelve years old, I was home alone when I found one of our cows bogged in a snowdrift at the bottom of a coulee, where a stream running under the snow had hollowed it out. The long-horned cow was in a place where my saddle horse was unable to get a good enough footing on the slippery, sloping ground to pull her out. So I went home and came back with a team, double trees and a chain. Fastening the chain around her horns, I quickly skidded her out onto firm ground, whereupon I went to take the chain off her head. But she got up like a flash, breathing fire and smoke and charged me. I dodged and she swapped ends to take another pass at me. I sidestepped her again and she went barrelling back out onto the drift, where she broke through, and there she was in the same jackpot as before. In the meantime, the team had spooked and had run home leaving me with nothing but my bare hands.

I was low in spirit as I trudged after the team, feeling bitter about cows and their intelligence, and muttering words that would have caused my mother to wash out my mouth with soap had she heard them. But I was also ornery enough myself to go back for another try. It was a long afternoon, but I finally got that nasty old blister of a cow out of her predicament, while learning something in the process.

The influx of homesteaders taking up land spelled the end of the old days of wide open country and free range. Periodic hard winters also took a toll, sweeping across the plains about every ten years in a freezing hell, with drifting snow that wiped out many of the biggest ranchers. Those who survived learned the necessity of having enough feed stacked up for winter use.

The ranchers coped with the need for titled land by having various members of their crews take up homesteads, proving up on them and then selling them to the ranch. It was a questionable practice in law but overlooked. They also bought land from bona fide homesteaders who had become discouraged. The railways had been allotted huge tracts of land by the government to encourage the heavy investments required to build lines across the vastness of Canada, and many ranches added to their holdings by buying from them as well, sometimes at a price of as little as a dollar and a half per acre. Others had large leaseholds rented from the government. But the number of really big ranches was relatively small.

Their problems were compounded, for they were faced with building and maintaining hundreds of miles of barbed wire fences. This was something most of the oldtime cowboys hated with a passion, for not only did it require much work on foot but their horses knew nothing of wire and many were crippled by running afoul of it.

One oldtimer who worked as foreman on one of these big outfits remarked, "For sure there's some satisfaction in ramrodding a big spread, but there's always problems and they're always big ones. It seems like you get one big problem taken care of and there's another waiting for you."

Cowboys and Horses

GIVEN TIME AND EXPOSURE, it didn't usually matter how green a man was when he started; he learned to cope with the cow country environment and generally acquired enough skill to hold down a job.

One young Englishman got a job on one of the ranches, but didn't last long. He was sent to a holding pasture to cut out eleven four-year-old steers and came back with four ancient cows. He was quickly looking for another job. When somebody asked him what had happened, he explained, "I couldn't remember whether the boss said eleven four-year-olds or four eleven-year-olds. I made a bit of an error, you see. By Jove, he was frightfully unreasonable about it! He fired me!"

My grandfather hired a young man from Toronto who came to the ranch looking for a job. He was the son of a manufacturing tycoon and very enthusiastic, but of course very green. He was, as grandfather put it, "so green that a cow would likely have chewed on him if he'd stood still in one place too long." He was relegated to being general chore boy and one of the first jobs grandfather gave him was to grease the wagon. He came back with the empty grease tin a half hour later to report that there wasn't enough grease—there had only been enough, he said, to do the seat!

Another day, he was instructed to dig a hole for a new gatepost at the corral. "Be sure to dig it good and deep," grandfather told him, as he rode out to bring in some horses. The horses were hidden and the ride was somewhat longer than expected. When my grandfather came back, dirt was still flying out of a large hole in the sandy soil and his employee was just about out of sight. "It would have been alright if my post had been long enough," my grandfather remarked in recalling the incident years later. History does not report whether this one ever graduated to being a cowboy.

Cowboys are a physically tough breed and it is generally recognized that it is hard to kill one. An oldtimer remarked that about the only way to be sure was to cut off his head and hide it someplace where he couldn't find it. Certainly they have survived some awesome injuries.

One, Guy Pallister by name, was helping load some big beef steers at Cayley, Alberta, in 1907. The crew had loaded a box car and Guy was putting the "bull bar" across the door when a wild steer broke loose and struck him. The sharp horn opened him like a knife and when the dust settled there was Guy all doubled up trying to hold his insides in with his hands. The train engine was ready to go, so the cowboys loaded him into the caboose and they headed for High River. There the doctor rearranged Guy's innards and sewed him up. By spring he was back working for the Oxley Ranch. He later married and when he died in 1958, at age 85, he was survived by ten sons and three daughters.

Toughness ran to personality and violence on occasion. When the Mounted Police came west in 1874, the first duty they performed was to close the whiskey trading Fort Whoop-up on the St. Mary River. Two of the traders, Dave Akers and Tom Purcell, went into partnership in a ranching venture, but eventually quarrelled and split up. Dave Akers eventually relocated on a homestead up on Pothole Creek a few miles from its confluence with the St. Mary River, where my grandfather's ranch was located.

The broken partnership did nothing to smooth relations between these two frontier hardcases, and when they were in their cups at various bars, they both vowed to kill the other. Both were always armed wherever they went on the prairie, and Dave was particularly watchful, for he was afraid of Tom.

At daylight one spring morning, Dave was saddling a horse in his corral when Tom showed up suddenly, riding into the corral through the open gate. Cursing and calling Dave every bad name he could lay his tongue to, he rode at him with a heavy elk horn quirt reversed in his hand ready to strike. Dave was not carrying a gun, but he hastily backed up toward a corral post behind which he had a .44 Winchester rifle cached. He grabbed the rifle, dodged a blow of the clubbed quirt, levered a cartridge into the barrel and fired. The bullet caught the attacker in the flank and emerged at the base of his neck, killing him instantly. Dave knew he was in deep trouble.

My grandmother was alone in the house making breakfast that morning when she heard a knock at the door. Upon opening it, she saw Dave Akers, who announced without preamble, "I shot Tom Purcell!"

"You shot Tom Purcell," she exclaimed. "Is he dead?"

"Christ yes, missus!" Dave assured her. "He's deader'n hell!"

My grandmother called grandfather, who was doing chores, and Dave told him that he wanted to give himself up. So grandfather hitched up a team and drove him to the Mounted Police detachment in Lethbridge, where he was taken into custody to await trial. If there hadn't been so much threatening, Dave might have gone free on a plea of self-defense, but as it was he was sentenced to two years at Fort Macleod for manslaughter.

There is a sequel to this story. Dave was married to a Blood Indian woman and she, along with numerous relatives, often visited him in jail. One of his jobs there was to clean, oil and repair police harness and on various occasions he slipped a piece of the harness to his blanketed visitors to be hidden and smuggled out of the fort. When Dave got out with some time off for good behavior, he had a complete, new set of harness for a four horse team. Of course this was a standing joke among the Indians, who were delighted with the prank, and the story was told around their fires for years afterward.

My father told about a rancher who came into Alberta on a fast horse during the Wyoming range war between cattlemen and sheepmen. It was said that he had killed a sheepman in a fight, wherein self-defense was in some question. His relatives later trailed his cattle up across the boundary and he set up a ranch in Canada. For years this man was rarely seen that he wasn't heavily armed. He seldom came to town and was always suspicious of strangers. If he saw someone approaching at a distance on the prairie, he immediately headed at a run for the nearest cover, where he would wait to find out the visitor's identity. Needless to say, nobody was inclined to approach him within rifle range, unless they had very pressing business. He married and raised a family, but to the day he died as an old man, he was always nervous and watchful—probably afraid that relatives of the man he had killed would show up looking for revenge.

In 1890 Harry Longbaugh, a quiet handsome young man, showed up at the Bar U ranch near High River looking for a job. He was an excellent rider and had no trouble getting work with Herb Millar, who was breaking horses for the ranch at that time. Nobody knew that back in Wyoming he was known as the Sundance Kid.

One day as Longbaugh stepped off a bronc and pulled off his saddle, Herb saw something glitter. While Longbaugh was roping another horse, Herb stepped over to the saddle for a look and saw that the glittering object was a hacksaw blade peeping out from under the woolskin lining of the skirt. He knew what that meant, but asked no questions and kept his mouth shut about it.

At the annual roundups, Longbaugh was rated a top hand and was a popular cowboy. Nobody knew that he was also one of the fastest and deadliest gunmen ever to show up in western Canada. He stayed around for two or three years and was respected as a good hand and a law-abiding man.

But then one winter he went into partnership with Frank Hamilton, a bully who owned a bar in Calgary. On several previous occasions Hamilton had taken partners to do most of the work; then when it had come time to split the earnings, he had picked a quarrel and beaten them up, thrown them out and kept the money. He tried it with Harry Longbaugh to his sorrow.

Harry was behind the bar when the row started. Moving with the grace and power of a cougar, he placed his left hand on top of the bar and vaulted over it in a twisting jump. When his boots hit the floor, a .45 six-shooter had appeared as if by magic in his other hand and it was jammed into Hamilton's middle. The money was not long in changing hands. The cowboy backed out of the place, got his horse and promptly disappeared.

He headed south into Montana, where he contacted some old friends, Butch Cassidy and Kid Curry. They set out on a ten-year-long trail of holding up banks and trains all through the western States. Finally, hard pressed by the law, they quit the country heading for South America, where they proceeded to raise hell in a similar fashion. Eventually they were cornered by a contingent of Bolivian cavalry and went under in a blaze of gunfire.

Then there was Dave Cochrane, an enterprising rascal with a reputation for picking up just about anything that wasn't nailed down. He became a thorn in the side of Dr. McEacheron, a veterinary and manager of the big Waldron Ranch located on the North Fork of the Oldman River, when he took up a homestead right in the middle of the Waldron range. Understandably, no rancher and least of all the testy Doctor would be very happy with such a light-fingered individual in such close proximity. The neighbors weren't very happy about it either, for there was even some question as to the origin of some of the furnishings of his cabin. Among these furnishings was a fine big kitchen range, which has its place in history.

Sometime previously, while on a trip to Fort Macleod, Dave had noticed several crates of household gear the Mounted Police had received, but had left outside in crates as the building that it was to go into was not ready. Among these items was a brand new kitchen range.

Dave had been with the Force, so he knew most of the Mounted Police and freely wandered in and out of the detachment headquarters every time he went to the fort. In due course everything removable disappeared off the stove. A pail of water was thrown over what was left and it developed a heavy coat of red rust. There stood the derelict in the open without even its sheltering crate. Then Dave went to the officer in charge and inquired about "that old wreck of a stove out back."

"I didn't know there was an old stove out there," the officer replied. But when he looked he was convinced, and Dave talked him out of the piece of junk.

Sometime later the same officer visited Dave's homestead and asked about the fine new range that sat there in gleaming splendor. The loquacious Dave answered his query by reminding him of his gift. "I just fixed it up and give it some polish," he said. The officer sat a while thinking hard about this revelation, but there wasn't much he could do about it without making himself look like a fool, so he chose to leave things as they were.

In due course, the Waldron Ranch bought Dave out for a good price, which was what he had had in mind in the first place. Then he moved on and his trail drops into obscurity.

One of the best known and best liked cowboys ever to live on the Alberta range was John Ware, a powerful black man who was a great bronc rider and cattleman. "Nigger" John, as he was called, was originally hired by Tom Lynch at Lost River, Idaho. Lynch was there in the spring of 1883 buying cattle for the Bar U Ranch. He was short of men to move several thousand head of cattle home, when big, soft-spoken John Ware showed up, without any saddle or horse but looking for a job. Lynch hired him and produced an old broken saddle and a gentle horse for him to ride.

Looking at this outfit, John remarked, "Ah say, boss, ef you'll jest gimme a little bettah saddle and a little wuss hoss, Ah think maybe Ah kin ride him."

The watching crew of cowboys broke into delighted grins at this opportunity for some hazing and promptly produced a good saddle and a much worse horse. John stepped up in the middle of him and put on a show like none of them had ever seen by riding the mean, snaky cayuse to a standstill. Then he went to work.

It didn't take Tom Lynch long to decide that John Ware was an outstanding stockman and he cut out a herd for him to take charge of on the trail to Canada. John and his crew were crossing Montana when a couple of hardcase ranchers showed up asking to cut out some cattle of theirs which they claimed had mixed with his herd. John knew they were lying, but agreed to let them look through the cattle, if they trailed along with the herd until it was time to bed it down for the night. This they angrily refused to do, but John was coolly unruffled though adamant. Then one of the ranchers moved for his gun and like a flash John jumped his horse between them and knocked them out of their saddles with the heavy butt of his quirt. As the herd moved on, the two claimers lay knocked out on the prairie. When they woke up it is likely their heads were sufficiently sore to remind them of the folly of trying any more shenanigans—anyway, they never showed up again.

John Ware's reputation for fairness and built-in fearlessness grew during the years he spent in Alberta. He was also a fun-loving man and nothing delighted him more than a good joke. One time he was working on a roundup in the High River Country and when he rode into camp for a fresh horse one day, he noticed the night herder getting some sleep in the bed tent with one of his feet sticking out from under the wall. John picked up a rope, put the loop over the sleeper's foot and tied the other end to a stout tent pin. Then he proceeded to pound on the tent roof with the flat of his hand while yelling as though the end of the world was at hand. The nighthawk woke up in the midst of this bedlam thinking he was about to be trampled flat in a stampede and came out of the tent taking steps ten feet long on the dead run. When he hit the end of the rope, he came down full length and upon rolling over he saw nothing but John and the cook doubled up with laughter.

John Ware was a living legend for years until he was killed by a falling horse. He left behind a wonderful family, who carved their own niches in the Alberta heritage. He will always be remembered for the part he played on the frontier—a generous, fun-loving, big-hearted rider who understood cattle and horses better than most.

One of the most colorful and eccentric old cowboys I ever met was "Barbwire" Johnny Spears, who was born in Ontario in 1880 and moved west to Fort Macleod with his family when he was ten years old. When he was only fourteen he quit school and went to work. It is doubtful if Johnny ever knew the meaning of real fear, though, as he said, he was sometimes a bit scared and knew how to be cautious. He was still in his teens when he worked as rough rider on various ranches, breaking horses that most men wouldn't care to lead to water.

He showed up down on his luck one day at the Waldron Ranch, dressed in mismatched boots and ragged clothes, looking for a job and claiming he could handle rough horses. The foreman wished to be rid of this ragged, yet insistent kid, so he cut out an outlaw for him to gentle. He didn't even give him a saddle before taking his crew out to work some cattle, leaving Johnny alone in the corral with the horse.

"It didn't take me long to size up that old booger," Johnny told me years later. "He was meaner'n cat piss! He had a glass eye on one side and a chewed off ear, and the way he stood there at the end of the rope, chuckin' his head with rollers in his nose, I knowed he wanted to kill me!"

Johnny snared the horse's front feet and hobbled him. Then he tied up a hind foot to his shoulder and worked the old outlaw over with a cowhide that was hanging on the fence. When the horse stopped fighting the ropes, Johnny went looking for a saddle. All he could find was a packsaddle and a couple of stirrups that didn't match, which he rigged up with a couple of lengths of rope. He cinched the makeshift outfit down on the horse and tied an old sheepskin onto it for a seat. By this time the horse was just standing still waiting for Johnny to get on top of him.

But Johnny had other ideas and proceeded to find some pieces of scrap iron that he hung on ropes on each side of the saddle, low enough to swing freely. Then he untied the horse's feet. The outlaw went sky high when the heavy iron began rattling, and of course it pounded him unmercifully as he bucked around the corral.

"He weren't no fool," Johnny recalled. "It weren't long before he figured there wuz no profit in beating himself to death with that iron, and he come to a stand flarin' those mean eyes at me and just darin' me to get on top of him. This I was fixin' to do, but fust I went down to the creek and cut me a willer club about three feet long and an inch through. When I stepped up on him, it was easy to see he'd had lots of practice. Even with all that hardware beatin' on him, he went mighty high and crooked. I caught him a good lick over the nose with my willer persuader to remind him that this weren't goin' to be any Sunday afternoon picnic and he gave up. That crew was some surprised when I showed up ridin' him. At first, he tried to eat on me once in a while, but that willer done some more discouragin'. Pretty soon he got more polite and turned out to be pretty good at workin' cattle."

Johnny wasn't a very big man, but he was tough. Like most of his kind, he was soft-spoken and good-hearted. He was getting on in years when I knew him, but was still a lot of man. He trapped and rambled through the mountains for hundreds of miles every year. He was always welcome around a campfire because his stories were full of action and a wry kind of humor. Listening to him was like taking a firsthand look back at the wild frontier of the past.

The oldtimers' methods of gentling a wild range horse were largely of the rough and ready school of thinking: they were first halter broken, ridden enough in a corral to start them answering the rein and then put to work. But there were some men that used different methods.

Years ago, when I owned over a hundred head of saddle and packhorses used in a mountain outfitting business, it seemed that in spite of plans to the contrary I always had a few snakes in the bunch. One day a man showed up looking for work and claiming to have had a bit of experience gentling horses. He was about sixty years old, had a look about him of having spent a lot of time in the saddle, but unlike a lot of old bronc fighters, he showed no signs of being stove up. His name was Frank Moon and I hired him.

Next morning we corralled a bunch of horses and among them were two line-back buckskin mares—full sisters, strong, good looking horses that were ideal for mountain work. I had bought them along with thirty head of gentle-broke horses, but whoever had handled them had abused them and they were the meanest kickers I have ever seen—the cool, calculating kind that are really dangerous. My plan was to sell them to a pet food cannery, for if there is any horse that I hate to have around, it is a kicker. On a dude outfit they are dynamite in disguise, especially this kind; they just wait for a chance then let drive with one or both hind feet, trying to wipe a man out.

As I showed the horses to Frank, I told him about these mares and my plans for them, and also that he didn't have to work with them. He stood there looking at them and just grunted in reply. I left him and headed for the house where I had some desk work to do. About half an hour later he showed up at the door and asked me to come out for another look at one of my mean buckskins. I found one of the mares standing alone in the round bronc corral with a lariat on her head and the rest of it coiled neatly on the ground in front of her.

"This horse is plumb gentle," Frank told me and then to prove it, he walked up behind her, took hold of her tail and gave it a pull. Getting down on his hands and knees, he crawled under her belly by squeezing in between her hind legs and out between her front ones. Then he stood up, talked to her in a low voice and rubbed her ears. She obviously loved it. Hardly able to believe what I had been watching, I took a closer look at the hitch on her head. It was a simple nerve line hitch rigged in a way I had never seen before.

A nerve line is rigged to work on two pressure points just back of a horse's ears, where two major nerves come close to the skin, and is used not only to distract the animal from struggling but also to bring it under positive control. When not used properly, such a hitch can ruin a horse, but Frank was a master of the technique.

Next day he called me out to the corrals again and again he had the mare by herself, this time completely free with no halter or lead rope. He had a light buggy whip in his hand and laying it over her back, he spoke to her and she trailed along beside him like a pet dog. Taking her to the back of the barn, he opened it and took her through, commanded her to stop, walked around behind her and closed the door, then led her down the length of the barn behind a line of stalls full of horses and out into the open yard. There, it wouldn't have surprised me to see her make a break for freedom, but she seemed to be mesmerized. She followed him around the yard in a big circle before he led her back through the barn following the same routine of opening and closing doors.

The next week she and her sister joined my packtrain for a summer and fall in the mountains. Both were model horses, easy to catch and friendly, as was almost every bronc Frank trained. He had worked all his life on ranches, from Texas to Alberta, and as far as I know no horse ever bucked with him. I once heard him say that if you wanted to teach a horse anything, you had to know a bit more than the horse. He was living proof of that statement. He died in his late eighties and Alberta lost one of the finest horse tamers and trainers that ever worked in the west.

The great unknown in the ranching business has always been the weather. In early days, the cattle on the big open ranges were completely dependent on the rich, native grass that cured on the stem in the fall and could sustain a cow all winter, sufficient even to put on some fat in milder years. Some of the ranches put up hay to feed their cows in hard weather during winter and spring, but for the most part the cattle were ranged on the open prairies. But about every ten years on the average, a prolonged cold spell with deep drifting snow flying on a northeast wind caused some heavy losses.

Cattle were almost impossible to hold in such weather and often drifted with the wind for great distances. The thin-haired cattle trailed into Alberta from the south were particularly vulnerable and sometimes froze solid standing up. Sometimes a bunch of cattle would blindly walk over a steep cutbank along one of the rivers and pile up dead on the ice below.

It was at such times that the cowboys had some miserable rides and many suffered frozen faces, hands and feet. There were many epics of endurance recorded and one of the most outstanding involved a man, Bill Greathouse, who worked as foreman for the Wilkinson-McCord outfit located in the big basin among the hills surrounding Sounding

Lake in central-eastern Alberta. This ranch was managed by Bud Wilkinson. In 1903, he and his brother-in-law, Tom McCord, sold their land holdings in west Texas and headed north with their livestock. They loaded eight trains with their 3600 cattle, 200 horses and all their ranch gear at Canyon, Texas, and unloaded at Billings, Montana. From there they trailed north across the boundary into Canada and finally arrived in the fall at Sounding Lake, 500 miles from Billings, with their outfit.

It is long grass country and for the first few years they did well, but then the cruelly hard winter of 1906-07 struck, and like every other ranching outfit in the country, they were in deep trouble. By February the snow lay two feet deep on the level and deeper in the drifts, with the temperature at fifty below zero.

To add to their troubles, the ranch cook became dangerously ill and needed medicine. Her name was Mrs. Ellis and apart from being an excellent cook, she was very well liked by all who knew her. Determined to help her if he could, Bill Greathouse saddled a fine big, grain-fed horse and headed for Stettler, and the nearest doctor, a hundred miles away.

The record doesn't say what he was wearing, but at that time and place he was likely outfitted with long wool underwear, wool shirt and pants, two or three pairs of wool socks, Indian tanned moccasins and overshoes, angora woolskin chaps, a buffalo skin or sheepskin coat, a fur cap and buckskin mitts with wool liners.

Hitting a steady pace and likely keeping to high ground as much as possible where the snow wasn't so deep, he headed for the nearest ranch in line with Stettler. Upon reaching the place, he quickly told them of his intention, and changed his saddle over onto another fresh horse, the best they had. So he proceeded, changing horses four times. When he arrived at Stettler he immediately saw the doctor, and while the physician was putting together a packet of medicine with instructions for its use, Bill took his horse to the livery stable, fed it well and took on a big meal for himself. Without stopping to rest, he then stepped back in the saddle and headed for home.

On the way back he reversed the procedure, changing horses at each ranch until he came to his own waiting for him at the beginning of the last lap. He delivered the medicine in time and Mrs. Ellis recovered. He made the round trip of 200 miles in an astonishing thirty-six hours, through a vast, cold, wide-open, snow-blanketed country under conditions in which landmarks were practically invisible in the white-out and without hurting any one of his mounts. It was an epic of sheer guts and endurance. Of such men the northwestern frontier of the cattle country was made.

To get along with any kind of animal, a man has to relate himself to it and think like it, and the degree of his success will hinge on this ability. Because a cowboy utterly depended on his horses, he had to be able to look after them properly and understand their shortcomings as well as their strong points. Horses, or most any animal for that matter, are as individualistic as people, no two being quite alike in character and some being much stronger in personality and more durable than others. I have known men who could get more out of any horse than other riders, and some who could ride and work horses without trouble that others could hardly get near.

Jimmy Miller was one of these, and while he often stated that "Yuh can't ever trust the grass eatin' sonsabitches!", he had a genius for handling and working horses. Even when he was an old man, Jimmy rode horses that gave much younger cowboys some pause for thought before they stepped up on them. They were dog gentle with Jimmy, but something else when it came to strangers.

When I used to ride through his small ranch while trailing horses back and forth between our headquarters and a summer camp about ninety miles north along the mountains, there were two things I learned to avoid. One was sleeping in his cabin and the other was to borrow a horse from him. I learned both lessons the hard way.

His log cabin was absolutely loaded with bedbugs that Jimmy never seemed to notice, but which attacked any unsuspecting visitor in regiments. Just as soon as the light was put out, they came in hordes. After one such sleepless session, I always insisted that sleeping outside on the ground, even in the snow, was the only way I could get any rest. Jimmy must have wondered how my wife and I got along, but he humored my eccentricity.

I rode into Jimmy's ranch trailing forty horses one late fall evening and was catching a horse to jingle my bunch with in the morning, when Jimmy talked me out of it by generously offering to loan me his, which he kept in the barn. I didn't know his horses too well then, but that was a condition due for some illumination.

Next morning at daylight, it was frosty as I went to saddle Jimmy's "gentle-as-a-kitten" horse. He was a tall thoroughbred cross and he eyed me in the way he would have welcomed a visiting cougar. But by being careful, I saddled him without any trouble and led him out to the corral gate, booted a stirrup and stepped up on him. Whereupon, he let out a whistle like a spooked elk, dropped his head and tried to kick off my hat. He went out across a big flat, breaking wind like a string of firecrackers going off and winding up like a three-star rodeo bronc. He had me bucked off about four times, but kept stepping back under me and catching me again as though he didn't want to spoil the fun. I never had less than six inches of daylight under my pants, but somehow I stayed with him, although afterward I felt so beat up that I wished I had been bucked off at the start.

When I had corralled my horses and joined Jimmy for breakfast, he made out to be astonished that his pet horse would buck with anyone, but there was a suspicious-looking gleam in his eyes. Other riders who knew him agreed that you'd better have your hat screwed down tight when you got on one of his horses or you would likely catch cold looking for it afterward.

When the oldtime cowboys found reasons for celebrating, their inhibitions seldom held them in shackles and some of their escapades are still recounted around evening fires. Of some of the individuals who worked on the ranches and trailed with the roundup wagons, a whole book could be written.

Sam Howe drifted into the country in the early '80s in the dust of a trail herd from the south and stayed to become one of Alberta's best known cattlemen. When he and his crew rode into town anything could happen and quite often did. On one such spree in Bassano, Will Pender, one of his cowboys, overdid the celebrating and passed out so cold and paralyzed that everybody witnessing his inert form agreed that he was dead. Sadly, Sam went looking for a coffin and the best he could find was a banana crate in which Bill was tenderly laid out in state in the hotel parlor with a friend standing guard.

In due course, after something of a wake lasting all night, a team pulling a flatbed dray was brought and Bill's body loaded onto it.

With a long line of mourners following, the funeral procession started for the graveyard. On the way, it stopped near the edge of town to allow some stragglers to catch up, and at that moment an old friend jumped up on the wagon for a last look at Bill. He was so startled when the corpse gave a slight cough that he fell off backwards and promptly disappeared. When they reached the cemetery everyone was thirsty and stampeded back to the bar for refreshments leaving the body momentarily abandoned. At that point Bill miraculously came back to life and sat up to view his surroundings with no little misgiving and astonishment. Somewhat shaken, he hurriedly left in the general direction of the mountains and never came back. To the day he died, he never touched another drink of anything stronger than water.

For Sam, whiskey was the juice to celebrate a happy event and for washing away the tears of a sad one. When his friend, John Ware, was killed, Sam felt bad and sat down in the bar at Brooks to wait for the northbound train running from Moose Jaw to Calgary, where the funeral was to be held. Sam's private wake got a bit out of hand with time, and when he eventually got on the train he failed to note the direction in which he was heading. Sometime later, the conductor shook his shoulder and said, "Sam! Wake up! Where are you going?"

"Where do you think I'm going? I'm going to John Ware's funeral in Calgary," answered Sam.

"Hell, Sam! John was buried two days ago and we'll be in Moose Jaw pretty quick!"

Cowboy humor had its pathos sometimes but often it was dry and to the point. I had a fine dog once, a German shorthaired pointer. He had a great nose and was always using it to investigate interesting smells, and his interest in these was indicated by the attitude of his tail. This appendage had been cropped somewhat longer than usual to take advantage of a white spot that gave it a tag on its end. He carried it in various degrees of elevation and it shook in all kinds of vibrations.

Eddie Burton, my cowboy brother-in-law, was watching him as he investigated something in a bush with his tail standing straight out and wagging a bit. Without a flicker of a smile, Eddie remarked, "What did you do—hammer it in or cut it off?"

Cowboy humor runs from the sublime to the utterly ridiculous and more than one joke intended to die on the vine of a chuckle of the moment, has proliferated and boomeranged. A story is told about Seven U Brown, who was bossing the roundup near High River in the '80s, when the green kid of the outfit asked one of the cowpunchers who the boss was.

With a perfectly straight face, the cowboy informed the kid, "That's old Seven U Brown. You'd better watch out for him—he shot his wife."

The boy was flabbergasted, and after some considerable thinking about this dramatic revelation, he wanted to find out more, so he finally sidled up to Brown and asked, "Did you really shoot your wife?"

"Who told you that?" asked Seven U, and the cowboy was pointed out.

Next morning when Brown was lining out his crew for the day's roundup, he left out this particular rider, who had enough good sense to stick to his boss and say nothing till he was directed otherwise.

Seven U was riding a magnificent horse that day and he made a tremendous ride without even noticing his companion. Arriving back at camp that evening, he turned to the cowboy sitting his lead-weary mount beside him and asked, "Are you hungry?"

"Plumb starved!" admitted the cowboy.

"Are you tired?"

"Dead beat!" came the reply.

"Good!" said Seven U. "That'll damn well teach you to go around telling people I shot my wife!"

Boots and Saddles

THE DAYS OF THE OLDTIME COWBOY, the long trail drives and the round-ups on the great open ranges are long gone and have become a part of history. Except for a few small islands, the great ocean of grass which originally supported hordes of buffalo, and later the cattle empires, has been plowed under to raise grain. The cowboys and ranchers of today have adjusted their way of going to a different use of the land and also to different equipment.

One of the major changes is in the use of horses. The oldtime cowboy virtually lived on horseback and his mounts were often anything but gentle. If a horse stood still to be saddled and mounted, it was considered gentle enough to be put to work, even though it might blow up upon feeling the weight of the rider in the saddle. Today the average ranch horse is much better trained and thoroughly reliable, gentle enough for most anyone to ride who has any experience. Methods of training are more painstaking and far more technical. The rancher running a herd of 200 cows with the help of his family and maybe a hired hand wants nothing to do with a horse that has bad habits or holds up work by bucking.

In the old days horses ran free on the range until they were five years old before they were corralled, halter broken and ridden. Now the colts are kept close to the barn a large part of the time and gentled while still very young. They are accustomed to being handled when they get their first lessons under saddle at two or three years of age, and by the time they are mature enough to do a day's work, they have graduated from schooling that is high in patience. No longer can a rancher buy an unbroken cayuse for twenty dollars or a rough broke one for seventy-five. A gentle, well-trained horse is now an investment of several hundred dollars and a particularly fine rope horse can cost thousands.

It is nearly a hundred years since the first rodeo contest was held and the biggest of them all is now held annually in Calgary. In 1912 when Guy Weadick promoted and organized the first Calgary Stampede, cowboys gathered from all over western North America to compete for the prize money. It was the first big rodeo of its kind ever held in Canada, and has become a legend among such competitions.

Naturally, at that first Stampede, Canadian cowboys were out to compete for their share of the prize money, and the favorite to win the saddle bronc competition was Tom Three Persons, a Blood Indian cowboy and a really great rider. Alberta sportsmen placed some heavy bets on him, but when the time came for the competitors to gather in Calgary, Tom was languishing in jail for some lighthearted misdemeanor committed while under the influence of firewater. This was a most undesirable state of affairs and the commanding officer at Fort Macleod was fully aware of the disappointment of all concerned. So he let Tom go in the custody of two policemen who escorted him to Calgary. Tom drew a good horse which he rode to a standstill in his usual showy fashion, winning top money. Then he was duly escorted back to jail to finish his sentence.

The Calgary Stampede now draws over a million guests a year and attracts more than a thousand competitors. Unlike their happy-go-lucky, reckless forbears, these young cowboys are serious, responsible athletes and sportsmen—which is understandable when entry fees run to considerable cash and a good man can win from $30,000 to $50,000 over a given rodeo season.

Although most modern rodeo competitors are in one way or another connected with the ranching business, it is possible for a city raised boy to break into the winning ranks by sticking to his objective and by learning the techniques in rodeo school. They start young. Only a few days ago I saw an eight-year-old boy draw a big, snaky cow in the amateur competition of a local rodeo and fit a prize winning ride on her. She was the female equivalent of a Brahma bull and no rocking chair. This youngster was ranch born from a long-time rodeo family; trained and toughened by practice, he will some-day be a great competitor in senior ranks.

The rodeo has always had competitions for cowgirls. In early rodeos, there were cowgirl bronc riding competitions and relay races. They rode the broncs with their stirrups tied under the horses' bellies and wore long heavy skirts. Because of the hazards of the competition and the tied stirrups, the incidence of injury was high and too many were injured—a few even killed—so this was stopped. Now the girls compete in barrel racing, a popular event with the spectators.

Rodeo is very definitely a part of the social life of ranching families. There are more people riding for pleasure, in competition and on working ranches today than ever before.

While in the old days the cowboys often rode many miles to compete in rodeo contests, or put their horses on a train to get to their destinations, now there is a horse trailer parked in almost every horse owner's back yard. Many competing cowboys and cowgirls pull their trailers thousands of miles in a season. Some of them fly and rent a horse they know from a friend when they get to a rodeo. Even when there is work to be done on a distant part of a ranch, horses are usually moved by vehicle to the scene of operations thus saving many tiring hours for all concerned.

To be sure, the activities and problems of horsemen and ranching have been altered by time and circumstances, but not all has been lost. Some of the atmosphere, life-style and conditions are very much the same now as they were a century ago.

The unique western saddle, a product and development of North America, designed for the conditions of work found there and reflecting to a considerable degree the needs of individuals with a flair for fitting the tool to the trade, is still basically the same. But the styles have changed. In the early days of the cattle industry various saddle makers, working out of shops located from Omaha to Fort Worth and from San Francisco, Portland and Great Falls to Calgary, turned out handmade saddles in the distinctive styles of their territories. A saddle made in Arizona was different from one made in California. Some of the old brand names were Visalia, Fraser, Mueller, Miles City, Porter, Hamley, Great West, and Riley McCormick, and they were all handmade to the last stitch. Cowboys have always favored saddles made from leather of the thin-haired steers of the south, because it wears better and is stronger. The best leather ever used by saddle makers was likely that from California tanned by the hand-laid, oak bark process, for it was very hard wearing and took the hand carving in beautiful detail as well as being a rich russet in color. Such a saddle would last a lifetime if properly cared for. Hanging in barns and tack rooms on Alberta ranches there are saddles originally made in California, Arizona, Texas and Oregon sixty and seventy years ago, and they are still handsome and usable today.

Most of the cowboys riding the ranges in early days favored for their work the so-called slick fork rigging with high dally horns and five- and six-inch cantles. Because there was no swell on the fork, they rode with a long stirrup by balance. But about the end of World War I, saddles began to appear with swells to hold a rider down; bronc saddle styling took a radical change with swells eighteen inches wide on some models and cantles seven inches high. It was like sitting in a box with the sides cut out and these highly specialized rigs were referred to as "bear traps." A strong man in one of these saddles could ride a bronc by sheer muscle power. Such outfits were frowned upon by really skilled, experienced riders, for they were dangerous if a horse fell. They were used for contest work, giving some advantage to a strong man. But then the cowboys, by mutual consent, adopted the well-known association saddle tree for contesting. A modification of this saddle with no horn is now used for contest work.

Ropers always favored a saddle that was easy to get out of, for accidents can happen when a rider ties onto a big steer or cow. If a horse gets jerked down out on the open range, the rider had better be on top of the pile or he is likely to get hurt. With the advent of contest roping, the style of these saddles changed to allow for fast dismounting, which can mean the hundredths of a second that spell the difference between hundreds and zero dollars in prize money. Although these low, slippery saddles are "leaky" when used on a bucking horse, most working cowboys on the ranches use them for everyday work now, for they are very comfortable.

Today it is no longer possible to tell where a cowboy comes from by the kind of saddle he rides. Not only are the styles standardized according to the work being done, but saddles are to some extent mass produced. The leathers are die cut and stamped with a design in the same operation, and trees are being made from fiberglass instead of wood. About the only handwork is in the assembly. However, the best saddles are still handmade throughout.

Fifty years ago, a hundred dollar saddle was mighty handsome, but today the same grade sells at $500 to $800, the variation depending on the decorative finish and extra frills. The highly decorative show saddles are worth thousands of dollars, but of course these are not working rigs.

I recall an amusing incident involving Charlie Furman, an oldtime cowboy who was a fine roper and was persuaded to enter an old-timers' roping contest in Lethbridge by his famous nephew, Pat Burton. Pat was several times North American champion calf roper. He rode a beautiful palomino quarter horse stud that he generously loaned to Charlie. So Charlie got up in the low roping saddle, backed his mount in behind the barrier and called for his calf. Right on cue, the big horse came out after the calf like a shot out of a cannon. He almost left Charlie behind and he, being somewhat disorganized, missed his throw. Later he was heard to growl, "Damn a saddle with no endgate! I wuz very near left sittin' on six feet of air!"

The braided rawhide ropes favored by cowboys of the southwest in the old days are a collector's item now. Only a few are being made by people who specialize in braiding rawhide hackamore nosebands, headstalls and bridle reins. Some contest ropers still use the time-honored, long strand, silk mantilla lariats considered more lively than the common, hard twist, nylon ropes now so popular. Grass ropes are vulnerable to getting wet, which tends to make them as unmanage-able as wire and then limp as a dish rag when dried out. A nylon rope is much stronger at any time and not affected by getting wet, but hotter to handle; if it gets jerked through a roper's hand it is like holding a hot iron, with painful blisters being the result. Still, most ropers go barehanded so they can feel their ropes better and make their throws more accurate. With time, they develop skin like leather on the palms of their roping hands. As one cowboy remarked, "It used to blister, but now it just smokes a bit!"

A cowboy's hat is his talisman, the badge of identification, and while thousands of people who wear them never step up in a saddle, you can tell the real thing by what is under it. It is basically designed to turn the sun and weather, protect a rider's eyes, and keep his face and ears from getting scratched when riding through brush. No item of a cowboy's dress is more important to him; it reflects his character and his pride. It might be so beat up it looks as if stampeding herds of cattle had run over it, or it might be a hundred-dollar headpiece reserved for special occasions, but it is part of the owner and has the look of being most essential to his well-being.

Nothing is more depressing or aggravating than a leaky hat in a bad rain storm, unless it is one that sheds its dye as well. For years I wore a black hat, its trademark synonymous with quality. One summer I bought a new one, ignorant of the fact that the company had changed hands. The new management cheapened the product, no doubt riding on the old reputation.

I was trailing a bunch of horses across the Rockies and we ran into wet weather. For five days it poured down on us and I was most uncomfortable. Not only did my new hat leak but it shed its dye and by the time that storm was over everything I wore was black, including my skin. The dye that didn't stay with the hat certainly improved when it colored my hide for it was weeks before I resumed my normal color.

Western cowboy boots have always been unique in design—like the hat, the trademark of the cowboy. They are designed with a trim, pointed foot, a high heel to keep the foot from going through the stirrup and high tops. The oldtime boot had a deeply undershot heel, sometimes as much as two and a half inches high, and the tops were higher, reaching to a point just under the knee. They were designed to protect the legs from brush and also from snakes on occasions when the rider was on the ground. In those days a cowboy spent a minimum of time afoot, so the fact that these boots were uncomfortable to walk in made little difference. Like saddles, they were then completely handmade, but now the cheaper ones are put together by machine work.

Now they have a twelve- to fourteen-inch top and come in many grades from plain to fancy. The expensive ones come with ornate stitching stiffening the tops and some have inlaid contrasting colors of leather decoration. Most modern boots have lower walking heels, which prevent a sprained or broken ankle when coming off a horse in fast contest roping.

Cowboy clothing is snug fitting, cut specially for riding and working in the saddle. The popular blue jeans and western-cut shirts are designed for utility as well as looks. Here too, styles change and now it is almost impossible to buy a pair of rider's pants with the oldtime stovepipe leg that hugged the boot, did not catch on brush or collect dirt. The modern flare bottoms—so-called boot-cut jeans—are sloppy and not made for practical purposes at all. The demand for them does not come from those who work on the range.

No longer do cowboys generally wear the big, brilliantly colored, silk neckerchiefs knotted at the throat. These were originally designed for more than just decoration and were slipped up over the mouth and nose to filter out thick dust kicked up by a moving herd. Some enterprising gentlemen also used them for masks, when they held up a stage, train or bank. It was said that the infamous Big Nose George, an outlaw of his time, got small benefit from this camouflage, for it failed to hide his enormous "wind splitter." Most modern cowboys wear no tie, except perhaps a bolo string tie—a part of "horse" jewelry that has many designs and can be very expensive.

While the cowboys and ranchers today have adjusted to the requirements of changing times, many techniques of their work are still much the same, and the character of the breed still flourishes.

A Way of Life

THERE HAVE BEEN CHANGES. No longer does the cowboy or his boss spend the long hours in the saddle covering hundreds of miles of open range. Nor is the cow business quite so much of a poker game with the weather. It is a rare thing now for cattle to be caught starving in a killing winter storm. The ranchers know how much feed it takes to winter a cow and they work hard to keep enough on hand with some surplus to take care of the unexpected.

But the weather hasn't changed; it is as unpredictable as ever with winter cold and blizzards just as fierce. Where teams of horses hitched to bobsleds and basket racks were once the only way of spreading hay, now tractors and four-wheel-drive trucks are the transport on almost every ranch. Where it once took a man all day to feed 200 head of cows, it can now be done in two or three hours. But still, some ranchers keep a team in reserve for times when wheels are bogged by snow conditions.

Hay is no longer stacked loose in big stacks for it is too slow to handle; it is now baled, which makes feeding much easier and quicker. Thus, every animal gets its quota of feed per day with guesswork pretty much eliminated.

There are still a few of us around, however, who remember the old ways in the hard, cold days of winter. When I was growing up on a small cow and horse ranch at the foot of the mountains in southwest Alberta, there was a time when I came to know what it was like to work long hours in the bone-chilling cold. It was mid-January when a blizzard hit the country dropping two feet of snow. Then it cleared and the temperatures dropped to forty below zero. My father came down with flu and was flat on his back in bed. So it was up to me to see that the cattle were fed. I was thirteen years old.

Up well before daylight, I threw hay and oats into the manger in front of our big team and then wrestled the heavy harness onto them. Leaving them to feed, I went to the house where mother had a hot breakfast ready. Then I hitched up and drove to a stack on the other side of the ranch, picking up on the way an old cowboy who lived in a tiny log cabin with his wife and daughter. He was a tough, stringy old Irishman, by the name of Phil Lucas, with a crippled hand. Together we forked loose hay onto the rack and spread it for the cattle, while sundogs glittered coldly in the steely sky. Then we loaded the rack again.

That work filled the morning. After lunch we fed the cattle being kept close to the buildings, then I took Phil home. By the time the team was fed, watered and put in the barn for the night, the woodbox filled and the other chores done, the stars were out. At night I did more than sleep, I passed out. It seemed as though I had just closed my eyes when the alarm clock would cut loose. Sometimes I slept through its clamor and then mother would come to shake me awake.

The days were a blur of unending cold, tired muscles, creaking hooves and sleigh runners, and the steamy smell of the horses. One night the thermometer dropped to fifty-two below, but it didn't seem to be much colder when I went out next morning.

On the way to the haystack old Phil told me, "Your nose is freezing. You'd better thaw it out with your hand." I took a look at him to see that his beaky nose was white as bone. "Yours is froze solid," I told him. He felt it gingerly and cussed, "Damn if it ain't! Hard enough to peck holes in a board!"

I couldn't help laughing and he looked hard at me with sharp blue eyes past the hand that was holding his nose, in a way that shut me up. Then he chuckled and remarked, "We can still laugh anyway. Things could be worse."

Like almost every boy in the country, I had aspirations to become a cowboy, but this part of it I could do without. There seemed to be no end to the cold. Dad was up and around again, but too weak to do very much. I couldn't remember what it was like not to be tired.

Then one evening just as we were finishing supper, the house suddenly cracked. Dad went to the door and looked out. "It's a chinook!" he exclaimed. "It feels warm as summer!" Next morning it was forty above and water was dripping from the eaves. The temperature had risen about eighty degrees in fourteen hours. In three days the hills were bare on the south slopes and the stock was lazing about enjoying the warmth. The wind continued to blow soft and warm, and apart from a few short snow storms the back of the winter had been broken.

Winter weather in wintertime is one thing, but when cold and snow hold on stubbornly into spring and the calving season, the life of a cowman can be tough. In the old days on the open range the cows were pretty much alone when it came to calving. If one got into trouble and was lucky enough to be spotted in time, she got help, but much more often she was on her own. It was a stark matter of survival of the fittest. Consequently, genetics had arranged that they didn't have trouble nearly as often as the more pampered cattle of today. Vets were few and far between and such things as caesarean operations were unknown. It is amazing what a cow can stand and even more impressive how newborn calves manage to survive, though there is a preponderance of bobbed tails and cropped ears from being frozen in a bad spring.

I remember a miserable night twenty odd years ago, when our phone rang at midnight and a neighbor was on the line. One of his heifers was in trouble calving and would I give him a hand? I put on some warm clothes and tied on my snowshoes, for the roads were blocked by drifts. When I arrived at his place, it was to find him out among his cattle with his Land Rover. The heifer had a calf stuck in her pelvic opening with its front feet showing, and she was so spooky that he couldn't get her into the barn. A good-looking, strong Aberdeen Angus, she was in no mood to be pushed around. While I watched she lay down and heaved on the calf, but it was being just as stubborn as its mother and didn't budge.

I got a lariat and a short piece of sashcord, then sat on the hood of the vehicle, while my friend eased it up to the heifer. She jumped up and started to move off, but I got a loop over her head and snubbed her to the bumper of the truck.

Closer examination showed the calf's head was where it should be, so I looped the sash cord over its feet like short hobbles and pulled. Seeming to realize that I wanted to help, the heifer lay down. Sitting down and bracing my feet against her rump, I timed my pulls with her heaves and in a few moments the calf was out in the snow. I picked it up and put it on some dry straw, then turned its mother loose. While we watched, she went to it and began to lick it vigorously and before long it was up on wobbly legs and busy sucking a bellyful of warm milk.

Even there in the dark with snow spitting on the wind there was something wonderful about it—an inert, wet, little thing suddenly blossoming into life and responding to its mother's care. The tired lines of my friend's face softened and smoothed out as he watched. "He'll make it now," he said. "Let's go have a drink. I got a bottle of Old Stump Blower for times like this."

Sometimes a birth can be a lot more complicated when a calf is coming backwards or has its head or a front leg bent back. Then it is hard work being a midwife—working with an arm buried in the cow's uterus against her straining muscles as one tries to rearrange the calf so it can get out of the gate of her pelvis. It is always messy and difficult, but heart-warming when it works out right. It is miserably discouraging when it doesn't.

In these times of high expense and low returns in the cow business, the ranchers work hard at all hours of the day and night to save every calf they can. Family teams work in shifts, so the cows have someone watching them closely almost every hour of the day and night, particularly in bad weather. There are vets on call to help with complicated cases. The survival of the fittest is not the rule any more.

After a miserably cold, wet spring, it is particularly pleasant to ride out at last across green meadows, warm under the sun, among contented cows with new calves at their heels. Their old winter hair is slipping; they are "slicking up" and there is lots of milk for the calves. Sometimes this promotes scours, which can be a virulent intestinal infection that will kill calves. So even then the owner is watchful.

With the coming of warm weather, there are miles and miles of fences to repair and branding to be done. As always, the ranchers help each other with the branding. Now the cattle are worked in corrals, but the methods haven't changed much. A roper still heels the calves and drags them to the fire. There teams of wrestlers throw them and hold them down for dehorning, branding, castrating of the bulls, vaccination and ear tagging. Some outfits heat the irons with propane gas, but many still use a willow-wood fire.

The modern cowboy always has a vaccine syringe close at hand to administer an injection of antibiotics in case of infection and to immunize the cattle against such diseases as blackleg, brucellosis and redwater. Now practically every herd is treated against redwater twice a year. In the fall the cattle are chemically treated to discourage the warble fly.

When the branding is done, the cattle are put on summer pasture, sometimes on big fenced leases on the prairie or far up various mountain valleys. Salt is scattered and the bulls turned loose—generally one to every thirty or forty cows. While artificial insemination is being practiced by some ranchers, it is by no means universal, for it is a time-consuming and expensive process, not altogether practical in rough, brushy country.

On the bigger summer pastures cowboys are hired to ride among the cattle keeping an eye on fences and watching for rustlers, disease and predators. As in the early days, it is a lonely life, although now pick-up trucks and CB radios give the men advantages of communication and transportation such as their forebears never dreamed about. Many of the cowcamps even have telephones.

Meanwhile, back on the ranches hay is irrigated, and when ready it is cut, baled and stacked for winter feed. It is a time of long hours and hard work there too.

By the time the aspen leaves are turning gold, the cattle are rounded up, various herds cut out and then trailed or trucked back to wintering pastures. It is market time, when yearlings or calves are shipped out to feedlots or sold by auction at various sales centres to feeders who route them in the same direction.

With the return of winter, the whole cycle begins another revolution.

Some of the changes from the old ways have been immense. But ranching people are still as enterprising and adventurous as ever. They are at once innately conservative and yet the greatest gamblers upon earth—anyone who stakes his future against the vagaries of weather and markets has to be a gambler to the marrow of his bones. Ranching is a business that brings bank account riches to very few people; it is a way of life. It is a challenge to make the best use of the good earth without abusing it. It is an art in its dealing with animals, where one must mix a strong back with a wise head and a warm heart. It involves many things, from training a skittish colt to the careful study of bloodlines, from welding a broken piece of machinery to the intricate plaiting of a hackamore from thin strips of rawhide.

Above all, ranchers have to be practical. Their spirit has not changed even though the vast, open ocean of grass has gone forever. It is good to pause once in a while to contemplate how much we owe those oldtimers who blazed the trails and showed the way. They worked hard and played hard and through their sacrifices made it easier for their great-grandchildren.

Plates/Cowboys through the Seasons

The Half Diamond S Lazy U.

Previous page: At dawn the low arch of clouds that distinguishes a
chinook moves across the Rocky Mountains.
Below: Jim Chalmers, rancher.

Don Thompson, rancher and former champion rodeo cowboy.

March calving. A newborn calf, only a few minutes old, receives a first lick from its mother, while in the foreground two ground squirrels search for food.

Below: The Bar HD ranch, a good-sized spread in foothill country. *Opposite:* Don Thompson returns for breakfast at 6:30 after checking the cows expected to calve that day.

Ropers heeling their calves to drag them to the fire for branding. The roper throws his loop down under the calf's hind feet.

Heating the branding irons in a willow-wood fire.
Overleaf: The branding corral.

Harry Denning, rancher.

John Morrison, young cowboy.

Hot-iron branding.

Dehorning, inoculation and castration of a male calf is carried out
at the same time as branding.

Brand of the Quarter Circle YS Ranch. Where the hot iron has
touched the calf's hide, hair will not grow and the animal will
have an identifying mark for the rest of its life. *Below right:*
Robert Chalmers and his daughter Jackie, a graduate of a course
in range management, moving cattle in June to the summer
grazing land after branding.

Rivals square off for a fight. Sometimes two bulls are so closely matched that they can cripple each other. The rancher hopes they will settle the mating order before going that far, but, until they have, the fighting will continue.

Below: Driving cattle to the summer range—Einer Brasso, rancher and Calgary businessman. *Opposite:* Packing salt to the high grazing land. *Overleaf:* Ranchland in the foothills, June.

Saddle horses.

Horses graze outside the South Sheep Creek Cattlemen's Association stable. In the old days horses ran free on the range for five years before they were corralled and halter broken. Today colts are trained at a very early age.

Right: South Sheep Creek Cattlemen's stable. *Below:* A trophy saddle is not an artifact to be preserved as if in a museum but a treasure to be proudly displayed in daily use.

Grooming horses is a part of a cowboy's daily chores.
Right: Clarence Boggs shoes his horse. *Overleaf:* Blacksmith Gid
Garstad—preserving an ancient trade.

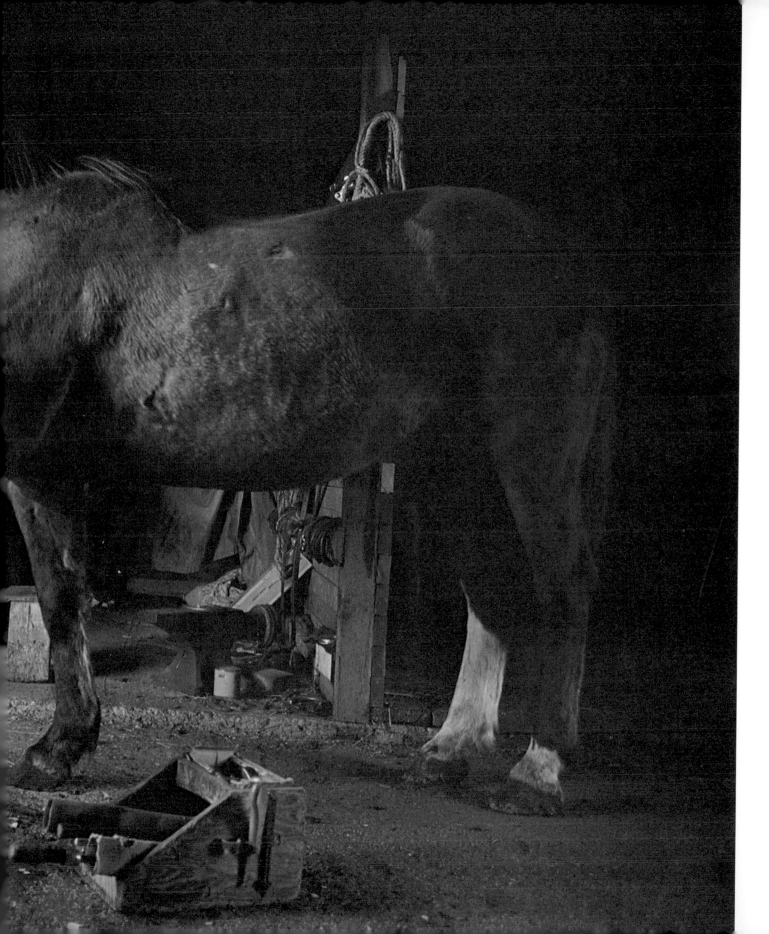

Hands on the horn of a working saddle.

Hand-forged steel, sterling silver inlaid spurs. Some cowboys also had silver on their bits, hats and buckles—enough to be seen miles away.

Below: Gold inlaid, sterling silver belt buckle. *Right:* The eight-second ride in fine style at the saddle bronc competition, Calgary Stampede. The rider attempts to stay on the "hurricane deck" for the required eight seconds.

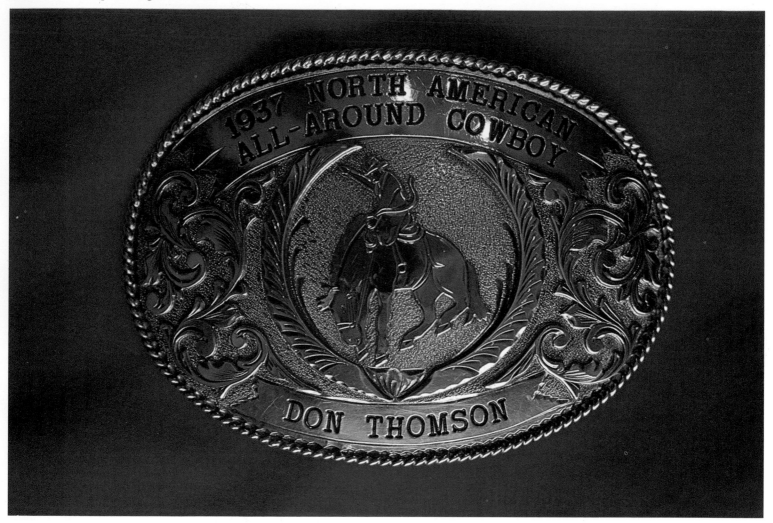

Bareback riding, Calgary Stampede. Sitting up on a snakey little
horse, and with hat and chaps flying, the contestant grips the
"riggin" (the band encircling the bronc's middle) with one hand.
To earn points, a bareback rider "rakes" the horse with his spurs.

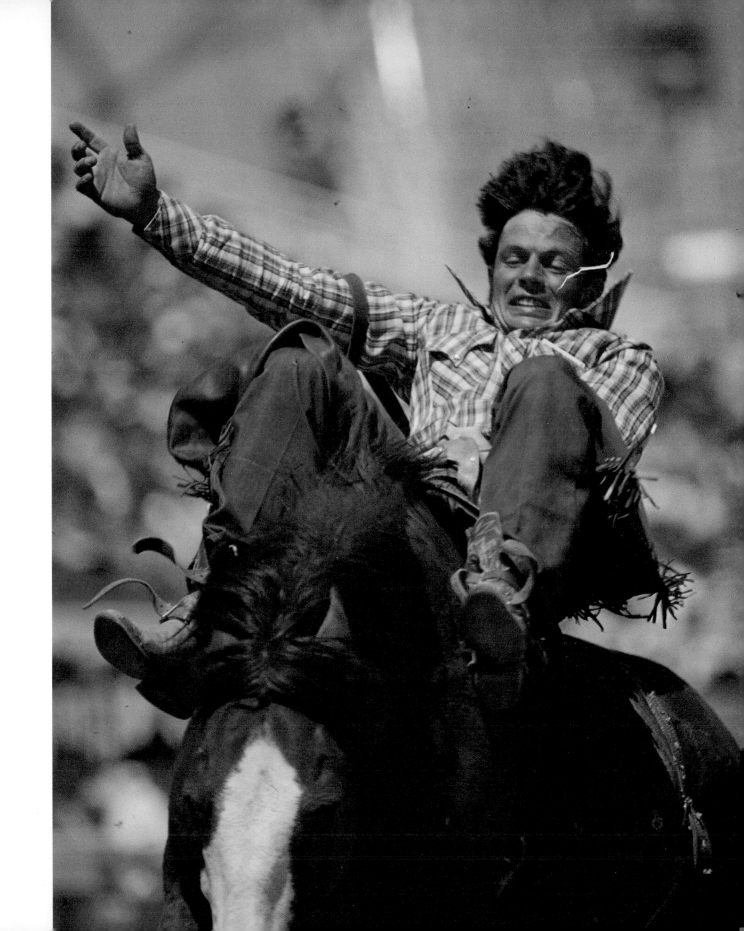

Right: Steer bulldogging. *Below:* Hung up. The rider's hand is trapped. A bystander and two pickup men are rushing in to bring the horse under control.

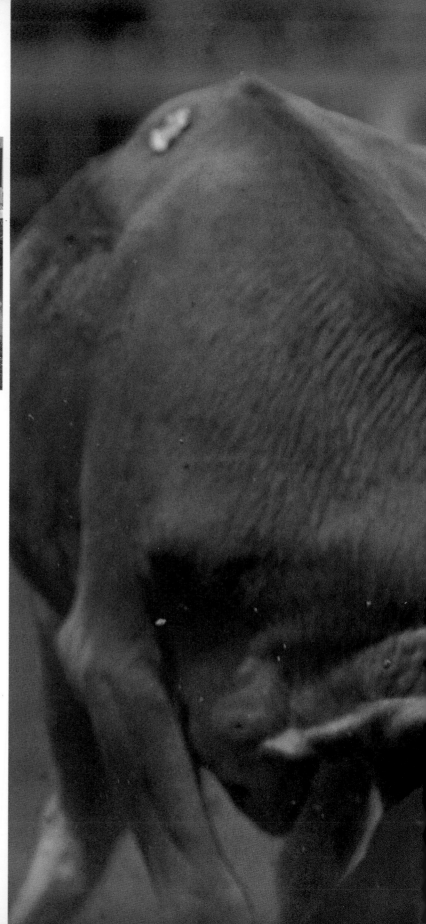

A rodeo cowboy sets his stirrups for the saddle bronc competition.

Coming off the hard way in the saddle bronc competition.

Opposite: Calf roping competition. Tom Ferguson, World All-Round Champion Cowboy, displays the skill that enables him to rope and hogtie a calf in six seconds. *Below:* Bulldogging competition. A cowboy leaps from his horse to wrestle the steer to the ground. The hazer guides the animal towards the contestant while the timer holds his flag up. *Two following photographs:* Chuckwagon racing, Calgary Stampede.

Pages 148 and 149: Fall roundup. Saddling up at daybreak.
Left and below: In the high grazing country during roundup.

Right: Moving cattle to the bedding ground in the late afternoon. *Below:* Prairie grass. *Overleaf:* Cattle trail heading for the low country.

South Sheep Creek crossing.

A saddle-weary Garry Thompson stops on the drive to warm his feet.

A break on the trail.

John Thompson moves cattle into the cutting ground, an area where the cattle of each ranch are separated from the full herd.

Cutting a steer.

Coffee brewed over the open fire.

Lefty Leflar, rancher.

Opposite: Del Brassard, cowboy. *Below:* Alec Murdoch, roundup boss.

The morning after the night before.

"Riding tall"—Alex Hartell. *Pages 168 and 169:* John Thompson, lead man. *Pages 170 and 171:* Cowboy Eddy Behm, 4'8" tall and 82 years old, still rides.

Previous page: The bunkhouse before dinner at noon. *Below:*
Albert Sandeman, rancher. *Opposite:* Horseplay outside the
bunkhouse.

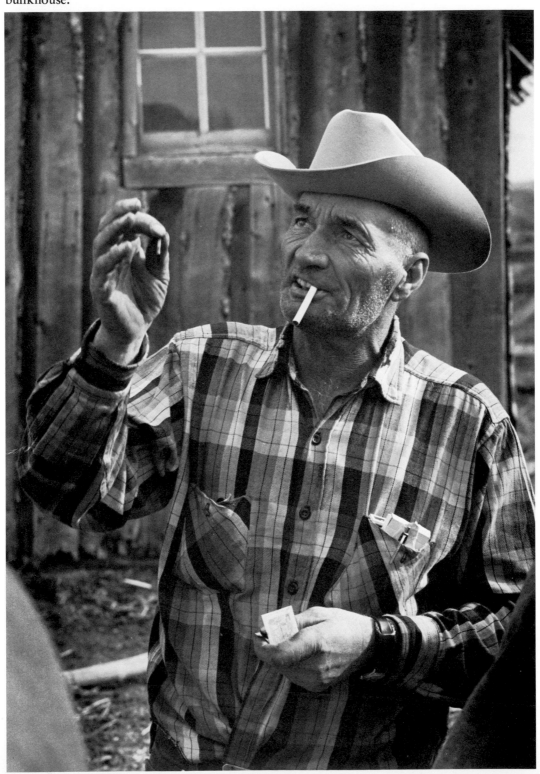

Don Thompson, President of the South Sheep Creek Cattlemen's Association.

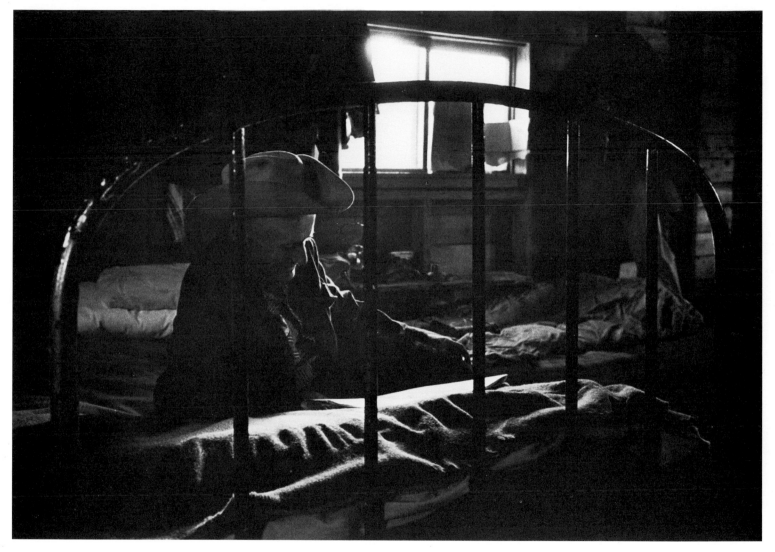

First snow, late fall. The "flunkie" chops wood for the cookhouse
and bunkhouse stoves.

Searching for strays. *Overleaf:* The last cattle are moved to the winter range.

Right: A corral at the home ranch. *Below:* Branding the "slicks," calves that were missed during the spring roundup. *Overleaf:* Arriving home.

A quiet drink, a game of cards and a story or two in the evening.
Right: Arthur Silvester, cowboy.

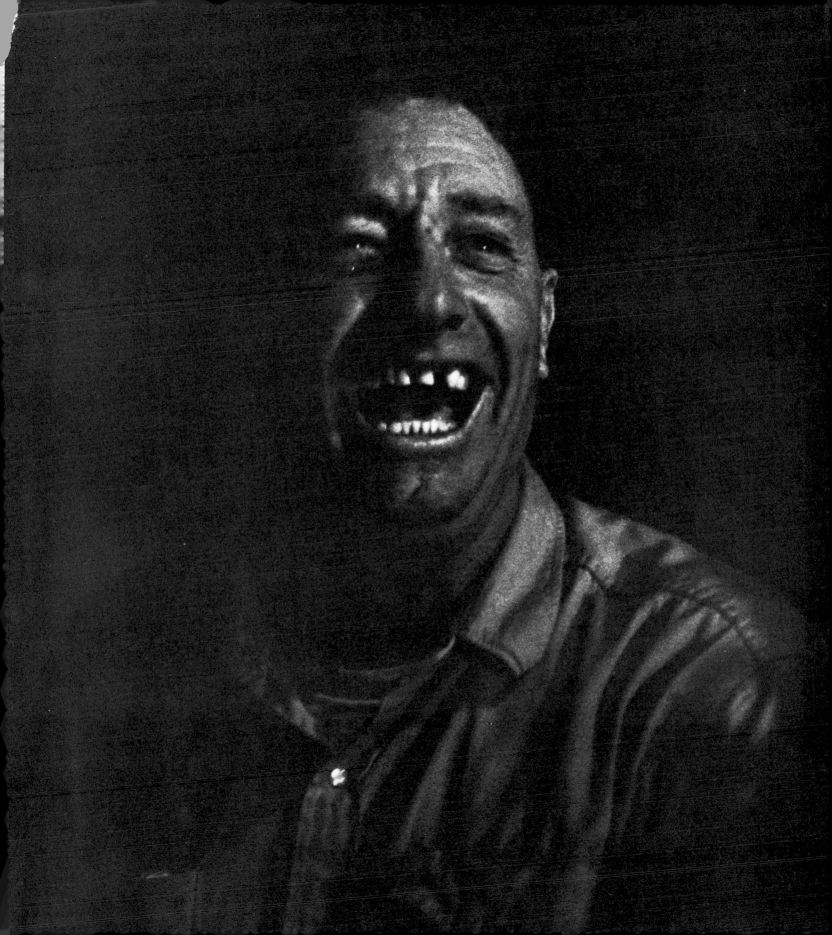

A well-earned rest. Most oldtimers would think it bad luck to place a cowboy's hat on his bed.

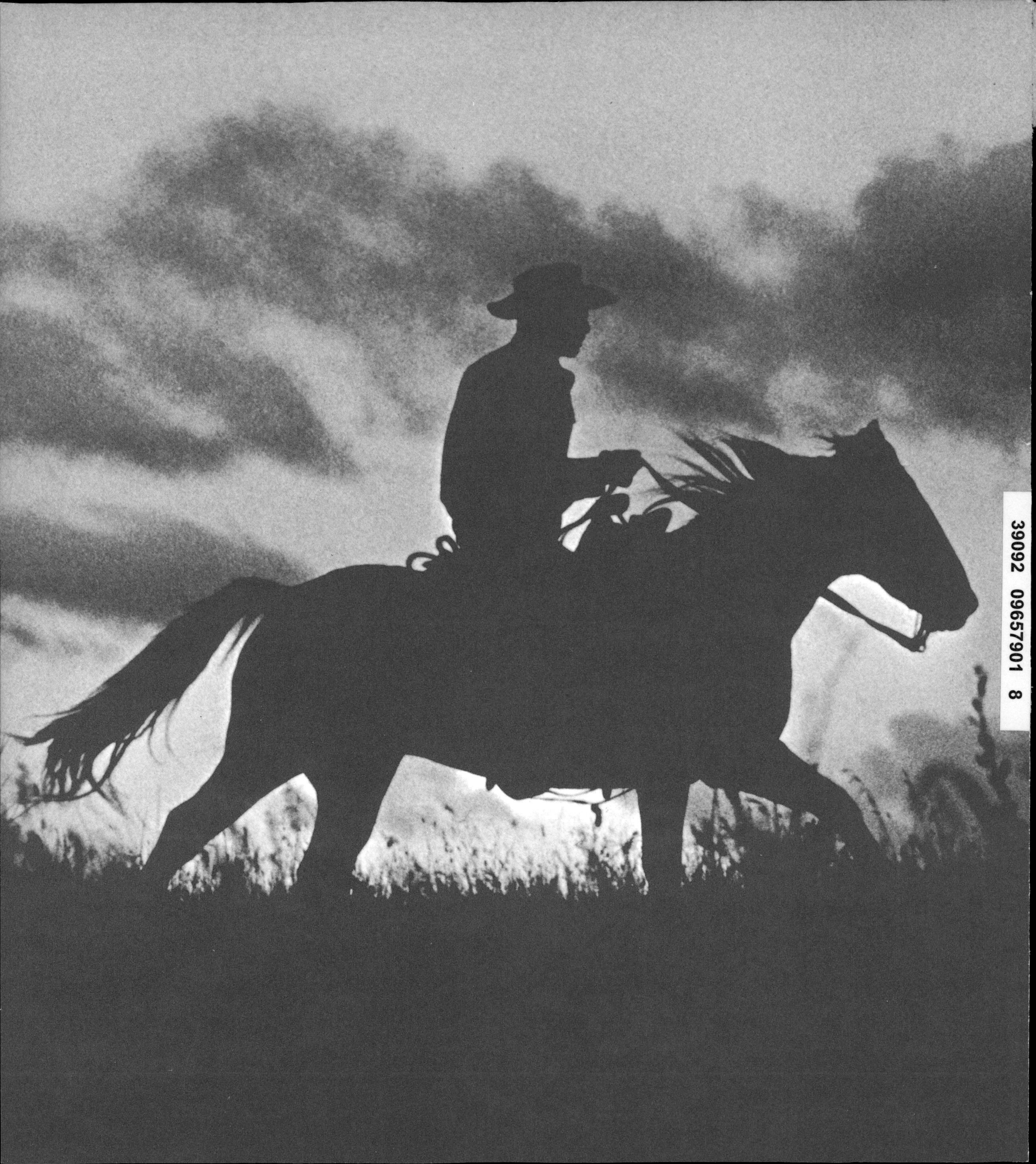